Other People's Dirt

Other People's Dirt

A Housecleaner's Curious Adventures

Louise Rafkin

Algonquin Books of Chapel Hill   1998

For generous support without which this book would not have been possible, I thank the Fine Arts Work Center in Provincetown and the National Endowment of the Arts.

Published by
Algonquin Books of Chapel Hill
Post Office Box 2225
Chapel Hill, North Carolina 27515-2225

a division of
Workman Publishing
708 Broadway
New York, New York 10003

Library of Congress Cataloging-in-Publication Data
Rafkin, Louise, 1958–
    Other people's dirt : a housecleaner's curious adventures /
by Louise Rafkin.
        p.   cm.
    ISBN 1-56512-162-7 (hardcover)
    1. House cleaning.   2. House cleaning—Humor.
3. Rafkin, Louise, 1958–   .   4. Women cleaning personnel—
United States—Biography.   I. Title.
TX324.R34   1998
648'.5'092
[B]—DC21   97-43673
                                                       CIP

Parts of this book have appeared in slightly different form in *The New York Times Magazine*, *The Utne Reader*, *Out*, *Los Angeles Times Magazine*, *Provincetown Arts*, *Tricycle*, and *Cosmopolitan*.

10 9 8 7 6 5 4 3 2 1
First Edition

Nobody notices what I do until I don't do it.
— Sign on the fridge at a house where I was
fired for leaving two Cheerios in the sink.

• • •

*There is no way to stand firm on
both feet and escape trouble.*
—The Odyssey

Contents

Other People's Dirt

007 or 409?
A Housecleaner's Humble Beginnings

Dear guest, will you be vexed at what I say?
—The Odyssey

I wasn't a particularly tidy child. I never envisioned myself wiping other people's fridges, having a preference for a particular paper towel, or carrying a personal vendetta against stray pubic hair. I was one of those gifted, slightly precocious kids, extremely curious, normal in some ways. I kept tortoises. I was a Girl Scout.

In the Girl Scouts I earned badges quickly and without much effort. There were badges for pathfinding and painting, letter writing and swimming, each a colorful round patch embroidered with an enigmatic symbol.

There was a badge for housekeeping. The stated purpose of the housekeeping badge was to "learn the things that must be done to keep a home pleasant, clean, and safe." I demonstrated correct use of cleaning implements —mop, vacuum, and broom—and executed both proper bed making and streakless window washing. I had to understand laundry sorting and money management, and I had to comparison shop for groceries. The patch itself was plain and uninteresting: a green field with a pair of crossed skeleton keys (a foreshadowing of the keys to the houses I now carry on my cleaning rounds). The patch should have featured a pair of shackles instead; this regime was perfect preparation for a position as the ideal postwar wife.

Nevertheless, in January 1968, when I was ten, troop leader Velma Bufford signed off on all eight of the official Girl Scout requirements, and I became a Certified Housekeeper.

But I really wanted to be a spy, and there was no badge for spying.

So I carefully watched *I Spy* and *The Man from U.N.C.L.E.* and Max and 99 on *Get Smart*. After reading Louise Fitzhugh's classic *Harriet the Spy*, I took to writing down everything I saw around me in the sparkling streets of my sprouting California beach town, just like Harriet in the book. I carried small journals clipped to my belt loop with braided colored plastic, a lanyard, which I changed regularly to match my outfits.

I painted a sign that read SINISTER SPIES and hung it on our backyard tree. Each day before walking my "spy route," I sat under my sign trying to convince myself that I actually could sneak *into* the homes I spied on rather than simply *peer* into them from behind palm trees or juniper bushes. But I was too good a girl, and couldn't bring myself to break and enter. Compared to the tough and fearless Harriet, I was gutless. Harriet hid behind drapes and climbed into dumbwaiters (a device my Southern Californian brain could not even imagine). I soothed myself with reason: after all, I lived in a world of Levelors.

And like every spy wannabe, I was least intrigued with the obvious. I spent time stalking people I thought were weird: the widow whose huge graying underwear flew daily off a line strung out her back window; the large Mormon family with a mother who fed her baby from her huge brown-nippled breast while walking around the house.

Actually, not much ever happened. I had little patience and hated to sit for very long on the prickly iceplant outside the widow's windows, so most of the time I made up stuff. I wrote in my spy book that the widow had been married to a murderer and that the Mormon lady was really nursing the baby of one of her husband's four other wives.

While I was busy trying to pry into the houses of strangers, interesting stuff was happening right close to home. One day I walked into my older brother's apartment to find Hefty bags full of sickeningly fragrant Thai sticks stacked on the floor like throw pillows. Oddly, I thought these mounds of marijuana were quite normal, and returned to spying on the widow.

Eventually the widow noticed me skulking around her house. One day, as I was sauntering out of the bushes on her side yard, attempting to look casual, she offered me my first cleaning job. Two hours after school two days a week for a dollar an hour. A way in! Although I did discover that her late husband had been a dentist (a perfect occupation for a murderer, I figured—all those drills and probes), the inside of her house proved no more interesting than what I had seen from the outside.

I also found out—unfortunately—that you can learn a lot about a person from washing her underwear. After a month of undies, I quit.

Most of us are taught to clean up, some by example and some by anti-example, by the folks from the "Do as I say, not as I do" school. I was raised in an extremely clean home; nothing was ever out of place, let alone dirty. "Clean up your room!" Although my father has been dead half my life, I can still recall the tone of his voice when he gave this order.

My father was obsessively neat. He sorted his golf balls into a row of shoe boxes: dirty golf balls on the left, soiled in the middle, clean on the right. My mother did two wash loads daily, whites and colors, and was always attacking a closet for a spring cleaning, no matter the season in our seasonless town. Our once-a-week housecleaner, Lupita, did the heavy work, while my brother and I were assigned gender-specific chores. I was in charge of the bathrooms and kitchen, he swept the garage and took care of the trash. Both of us have turned into our parents: he is a single dad whose kids suffer through daily room-cleaning regimes; I can't sleep if there is a dirty dish in the sink.

I knew there were others who lived differently, amid mess and dirt and grime, but even then I didn't understand it. I had a friend whose hamster lived in the kitchen; hamster poop pebbled the counter. The fridge at her house spawned stuff that might have started life in a petri dish. Trash cans in the bathroom overflowed with wads of tissue, nests of candy-striped dental floss, and matted yellow-and-brown cotton balls, like the fur off some dying animal. I tried not to eat at this house, which rarely proved to be a problem because eating necessitated unearthing a plate or a fork from under stacks of newspapers and piles of dirty laundry. Besides, if there was anything really edible there, the sometimes free-range hamster had probably gotten to it first. At a sleepover for this friend's birthday, I squatted over the toilet so that my thighs wouldn't touch the bacteria-ridden seat.

Her older brother, a tall, pimply, bookish guy, intrigued me. He did his own laundry and kept a lock on his spotlessly clean room.

He grew up to be gay.

In 1971, at the important age of thirteen, I somehow found myself in the running for Home Economics Student of the Year.

I had sewed an A-line skirt and demonstrated proper dishwashing order (glassware, silverware, dishes, then pots and pans). I had baked chocolate-chip cookies and produced the exact yield written on the recipe. I'd eaten a ton of dough but made the cookies the size of peanuts. I got an A in cookies. In class, I tried not to upset our teacher, Mrs. Maven, a pinched, finch-like creature who had heart trouble and, it was rumored, would die if she got angry. I'd learned how to polish silver and properly scour a sink.

It was the era of tie-dye, bell-bottoms, and free love—people even started to eat Chinese food with chopsticks. I knew if I won Home Ec Student of the Year, it would be like getting the award for being the biggest dork in the whole junior high. Of course, I was victorious. Dutifully, I wore the A-line skirt to receive my award.

"You'll make some lucky man a great housewife," Mrs. Maven whispered as she handed me a gold-edged certificate and then shook my hand.

"Nice work, Betty Crocker," said Kurt Higgens, who stood next to me on the awards platform. His certificate, for PE Student of the Year, seemed unfairly cool.

Once home, I threw out both the award and that skirt.

I was no Betty Crocker. I was a Feminist.

In high school I debated Phyllis Schlafly over the ERA. (Remember when ERA stood for a constitutional amendment and not a real estate conglomerate?) Everyone laughed when she said that the reason women should not be equal to men was because we would no longer have separate toilets. But she was serious.

"Do you want your daughter using the same facilities as a *wino*?" she asked my mother. My mother, sitting front row under faux chandeliers in a fuchsia and mauve convention room, could hardly have said yes.

"So you want her fighting a war?" My mother was frozen, caught in the headlights of the revved-up right wing.

I was enraged, ready to chuck my pacifist convictions and even my leather-thonged brass peace pendant in order to join the Marines Corps just to prove my point. Women's Liberation Now. Naively, I thought Phyllis was the only one I'd have to fight. I thought feminism was so entirely logical, such a darn good idea, that society would change instantly, like a mood ring. Phyllis's world of cooking and cleaning was passé.

What happened? History stumbled forward. The ERA didn't pass. The backlash lashed. Jane Fonda metamorphized from activist to aerobics instructor.

One after another, I took cleaning and waitressing jobs.

But I still hoped to be a spy. At college I signed up for an internship with the CIA. Interviews were to be held on campus the following week. I told my mother who told Bucky, my brother.

"You're not serious about this spy thing?" Buck's voice on the phone sounded frantic. It was 2:00 A.M. I could hear sitar music and people arguing in the background.

"Why not?"

My brother, who had now graduated from dealing Thai sticks to running cocaine from Bolivia, was just a tad concerned about the CIA's background checks. It seemed there were officials in Interpol who knew about his international commerce and jet-setting life, and they actually had let him know they knew. But the CIA was less gracious about such entrepreneurial self-employment. Following my dream to supersleuthdom would get him investigated and busted, Buck said. Besides, he added, a drug runner in the family was a credential that would hardly clinch me the internship, regardless of my perfect G.P.A.

I consoled myself: D.C. was humid and miserable in the summer anyway. I went to France.

Cleaning villas on the French Riviera sounds glamorous. However, to echo the sentiment of a famous expatriate: a toilet is a toilet is a toilet. I did learn that the French have a particularly pleasing and effective method for mopping floors. (Tie a damp terrycloth towel over the end of a push broom—works better than any mop on the market.)

Our cleaning crew was made up of illegal workers from England, America, Morocco, and the Netherlands. Each morning, our motley group—sunburned, hungover, and cranky—met in front of the corner *tabac*, where we were picked up in a van by some guy rumored to have connections with the French mafia.

Dropped off in pairs in front of various houses, we were given keys and a pickup time. We cleaned empty houses, rentals, changing them over for the new sets of rich tenants arriving weekly. The perk of the job was that any food or alcohol found in the house was ours. Apparently, monied vacationers did not wish to be offended by leftover butter or half-bottles of table wine. We, of course, were anything but offended by anything free. Half-eaten or gnawed food? No problem. I collected quite an array of mustards, tinned fish, and, naturally, wines. I learned early on not to get paired with either Pasquale, a sixteen-year-old Parisian runaway, or Franz, a forty-year-old perpetually stoned hippie from Amsterdam. Both would pilfer everything for themselves, guilt-tripping me out of my share of the goods. And neither one could clean worth a damn.

I partnered with Pip, a Brit, also a student. Pip was energetic and fastidious, and we always finished well before pickup time. We spent the extra hours watching TV or taking baths, a much welcomed luxury as she and I were both living in tents.

One day we were dropped off at a villa next to a Club Med. The house was already spotless and it was a really hot day. The Club Med pool beckoned from less than two hundred yards away.

People seemed to be moving freely in and out of the club compound, toting shopping bags and wearing large hats and sunglasses.

"Let's do it," Pip said. I protested, but only weakly. Though I still hated the thought of getting caught doing anything illegal, it was *really* hot.

Full of trepidation, I swung my string bag jauntily as I followed Pip through the Club Med gates. Minutes later we were cooled, smiling at each other over the hairy belly of a middle-aged man floating by. "And we're getting twenty-five francs an hour," Pip said "*Pas mal.*" She disappeared under the water.

Then suddenly we found ourselves being hustled into a darkened, disheveled room by two hunky, tanned French guys, wearing only Club Med staff sarongs. We faced them awkwardly in our dripping wet bikinis. Pip translated what they said.

"It's simple. We screw them and they let us go. We don't, they turn us in."

"Merde," I mumbled, demonstrating that I had learned at least one important French word.

"May-rd," said hunk number one, mimicking my poor accent.

One guy seemed quite shifty, possibly without scruples. The other one was nicer and told us he was some kind of song-and-dance leader. Both thought their offer was generous. They said they usually got paid to have sex: female Club Med punters, single or not, wanted holiday flings and, though the vacations were all-inclusive, *that* was extra.

I could tell they found us amusing. I crossed my arms over my breasts and longed for the safety of a dirty bathroom.

Pip looked at me. "Do *you* want to?"

"Jesus, Pip! Are you crazy?"

"Just checking." The guys looked at us smugly. One adjusted something under his sarong. I kept my eyes at head level.

"Pardonnez-moi," Pip said politely, suddenly making a beeline for the door. One guy reached out to grab her arm and she turned, spouting a vitriolic stream of French, something like "You lay a finger on me and I'll rip your flesh wide open with my teeth." Both hunks moved aside and I scampered after her, my hero. She was ballsy enough

to stroll back to the pool and casually slip on her shorts and hat before striding out through the front gates.

We hitchhiked home. The next day Pip found us waitressing jobs at a beachside restaurant. More money, shorter hours, free meals.

The hitch?

Serve topless.

We worked with a local woman who was doing the owner in the back alley. She kept her pen tucked under her right breast. I figured if you could tuck anything under there, it was time to quit.

After college I still hadn't a clue what I was going to be when I grew up. My unwieldy tongue never had tamed much French—save for what was absolutely necessary to delivering a three-course meal. Like many drifting graduates, I signed on for more schooling.

In graduate school I learned that teaching American literature and composition to gaggles of undergraduates was stressful and not very gratifying. Prospects in academia did not beckon. Jobs were scarce. My dreams of super-sleuthdom had receded into a romantic fog. Besides, spying meant finding out things but then keeping them secret. By this time I had figured out that the point of knowing anything was to tell it. I set off to be a writer and tell everything.

But there were fewer jobs for writers than there had been for teachers. My colleagues in the crowded world of aspiring Hemingways took jobs as typists and proofreaders.

Unfortunately, I never learned to type, on political grounds —"I'm not going to be any man's secretary!"—a bad move in retrospect. And I can't spell. Once I was frozen at the keyboard: I could not figure out how to spell *are* because logically I thought it should begin and possibly end with an *r*.

My cleaning life began in earnest eight years ago. While living on a scant writer's fellowship on Cape Cod, I had bartered my home ec skills for services: cleaning for massage, cleaning for chiropractic care. (A chicken-and-egg situation if ever there was one: first you pull your back out vacuuming, then you get it fixed—free!) At the end of the fellowship, which supplied room and board, I again faced the horror of paying rent.

I put up a sign at the local A & P. I provided the all-important pull-off tabs printed with my phone number.

"Cleaning. Responsible. Local References. Fast."

There it was. My name and right next to it, the word *Housecleaner*.

All of this is to tell you a little about who I am. Because, after all, as a housecleaner I'm the one who knows everything about everybody else.

Alone in a house, I piece together strands of life stories as if I were an archaeologist, the home a midden. I know who has sex with whom, and how often (condoms in the bathroom, stray hairs on the pillow). I know who is not having sex (separate rooms, separate beds). I know who has an eating disorder (Weight Watchers in the freezer,

pictures of svelte models and a string of diets rotating po-
sitions on the fridge door). I know the alcoholics by the
bottles tucked behind the bed in the spare room.

I watch people fight. Sometimes they want me to take
sides. *Uh-uh*, I say, and flip the vacuum on.

I know who tricks every night. I know who has $1.2
million in just one of their stock portfolios. I know which
wife is having an affair. I know which wife calls her husband "honey" and then, when he leaves, "the creep."

I don't read diaries but I read clues. I see things and I
hear things. I am there when the answering machine picks
up. I have heard rendezvous arranged and indiscretions
confessed. I dust birthday cards and fish behind head-
boards, all in the name of cleanliness.

Armed with a battery of house keys, I make my way
through a maze of homes, identifying clues and decipher-
ing dirt. Disguised as a pleasant, competent housecleaner, I
am invisible.

Who needs the CIA?

Heroes of the House

But I cannot recount or name them all:
the many wives and daughters of the brave.
—The Odyssey

Once I decided to do it, my foray into professional housecleaning happened quickly. It was on the very day that I pinned my cleaning flyer on the supermarket bulletin board next to the offers of free kitties that the blinking light on my answering machine presented the reality of my newfound profession. A gynecologist and his wife wanted an estimate.

The four-bedroom tri-level Cape Cod summer home was dusted with a yellow coat of spring pollen. Trailing the woman, I scrutinized the bathrooms and counted the bedrooms. I figured and calculated. Then I choked. I blew the estimate, offering my speed-demon skills at a price that I rightly figured would land me the job. As it turned out, I cleaned that home for an entire summer for about what her husband would charge for a single Pap smear.

During my first few years I made a lot of mistakes. Times were lean. I said yes when I should have said no. I cleaned for people with dogs. I cleaned for people with gaggles of kids, even babies. Actually, babies are fine. It's only after they try feeding themselves that the trouble begins. I developed this equation: If there's a toddler, there has to be a dog—the dog will surely shed but at least the food on the floor will be taken care of.

That first year I took on a woman who paid me in loose change and talked me down five dollars on my quoted price for the job, this while I stood in her new million-dollar summer home. I worked for a couple who routinely scheduled huge parties the night *before* I came to clean.

But I accepted my Cinderella role dutifully and without complaint. During most of my early years on the job, I was a wimp.

"Where's that damn prince?" I complained to my coworker A.J. one day as we were leaving the house of the "Loose-Change Lady." (Most of the time I clean with A.J. or another coworker, who vacuums while I do the wet work—bathrooms and kitchens. It's important to have someone handy to complain to, plus I prefer wet work. I enjoy spraying products meant to smell like the natural world—pine, citrus—yet still smell obviously like cleaning products.)

"I'm ready for that fairy-tale ending," I said to A.J. It had been a particularly bad day. Earlier, while I was on my hands and knees in the bathroom singing along with the song on my Walkman, Loose-Change Lady had tapped me on the shoulder. Signing wildly, she gesticulated that something was wrong. I moved my earphones aside and smiled wanly. She told me, "You're off-key."

"Fairy-tale ending?" A.J. challenged. "Cinderella ends up marrying some strange guy because of her shoe size and her sisters' evil eyes are pecked out by doves! They probably ended up freeloading on her the rest of their lives."

"You're right," I said. "She probably cleaned up after the whole lot of them—with her husband insisting she wear those uncomfortable glass slippers."

By accident, while reading a story to my niece, I discovered that despite his famous parentage, Hercules put in time as a cleaner. It was part of his penance for killing about six of his own kids.

As punishment, Hercules was given a set of tasks, one of which was to clean the Augean stables. They hadn't been cleaned for thirty years.

But Hercules didn't mess around with all that horseshit. He simply diverted two nearby rivers so that they ran smack through the stables.

Waves of horse manure swamped the flood plains, polluted endangered salmon-spawning grounds, and swept downstream into the backyards of some unsuspecting peons, but soon the job was finished. Apparently Hercules had better things to do than fret about the environment.

Although I was outraged by Hercules' selfish cleaning technique, my niece remained enamored with the macho hero. She did, however, come up with a sensible response to this fable: "Why *hadn't* those stables been cleaned for thirty years?"

Not surprisingly, there are few role models for responsible, strong-minded cleaners. As a kid I think I was only vaguely aware of a handful of prime-time TV cleaners. Beulah, the first black character to headline a TV show, and Hazel were the front-runners, living-in at the homes of wealthy white families. Later there was the wacky Alice who worked for the Brady Bunch, and the curmudgeonly Florence at the Jefferson's.

I never paid much attention to these characters. For the most part, they seemed silly and foolish. However, I did read and reread Peggy Parish's books about the simple-minded housekeeper Amelia Bedelia. When the overly literal Amelia was told to dress the chicken, she did just that, fashioning tiny clothes for the bird.

When I first began cleaning I liked to think of myself as a somewhat hip and creative version of Amelia Bedelia. I could only pull this off for so long. Sooner or later, reality was bound to set in. My personal transformation from meek and mild scrubwoman to maid with a mind of her own occurred organically, but suddenly. It was several years into my cleaning life, at a house where the client had never even taken the time to learn my name. At the end of our shift, he'd hand me a check with the line for the name completely blank.

I was relocating a pair of his dirty underwear from the floor to a chair by means of a coathanger. A.J. watched from across the bedroom, giggling.

"I don't move dirty underwear," I said to A.J.

"No?" she said, eyebrows up. "You could have fooled me."

Right then the man sailed in from the hall. "Change the sheets, would you?" Folded sheets in hand, he seemed baffled by my fishing maneuver.

"No," I said, the offending briefs dangling from the wire hook.

For the the right person, I'd pick up dirty underwear, change sheets, and even sweep up dead rats (and I have), but this wasn't the right person.

"No," I said again, having made the decision that this was a job I no longer wanted. "We don't change sheets." Obviously angered, he tossed the bundle of sheets on the bed and left the room.

"Unless you want them really changed," I said to A.J. once he had departed. "Like shredded."

A.J. laughed, I laughed, and we never went back there again. It was my first good riddance, though I did see this guy years later in a movie theater. He was sitting in front of me, and I knew, if I didn't move, I could never enjoy the film. I was afraid I would be recognized.

And afraid I wouldn't be.

Although few can imagine them, there are fairy-tale moments in a housecleaner's life, despite crabby clients and sometimes being treated as less than human. I have felt flashes of transformation along the lines of Cinderella's, and witnessed situations as dramatic as Hercules' clean sweep.

One such moment involved a sweet elderly client. An alcoholic, he was almost always tipsy. One morning he met me at the door in a panic; he had somehow misplaced $1,000 in cash.

"Forget the cleaning," he told me. (I hated cleaning this house—it was large and rambling, and the only joy was finding bottles hidden in new places, like the guest shower.)

"Just find the money!" he implored, and I didn't dare get close to him. The smell, even at a distance, was overwhelming.

Together we turned the house upside down. Eventually, I discovered the money stuffed into an empty toilet-paper roll buried in the laundry hamper. With the wad of cash in my hand, I found him on the living room couch, weeping. Sighting the green roll, he jumped up, took my arm, and insisted on leading me in a celebratory waltz. At that moment, strange as it now seems, dancing together was the only thing we could have done.

I was tipped a crisp $100 and was home before noon.

At another house, I found my prince—of sorts. I was side-by-side at the sink with a client, a Hollywood somebody, who had taken years to warm to me. Whenever I was there, he was usually absorbed in his work, a splay of legal pads covered with scribbled bits of dialogue before him on the dining room table. Often he was on the phone talking to someone I've only experienced through the pages of *People* magazine. While cleaning, I'd listen in on his conversations, imagining what I thought would be a Somebody's life—palm trees and personal trainers.

Fastidious, he hated that his stainless-steel sink was

stained. So one warm, sunny morning, I showed him the secret of sink de-rusting, and there we were, shoulder-to-shoulder, our elbows bumping, our muscles churning, swabbing the twin sinks.

He was amazed! Delighted! Rust stains, the great leveler. I imagined the advertisement: "Soft Scrub—even eradicates class distinctions!" And who could have thought that we, the two of us, from such different parts of the world, would share such a moment?

Often I just can't help myself. Once while I was dusting at a one-time-only job, I found a letter taped onto the back of a picture frame. It was unsealed and addressed to a man I vaguely knew. Of course, I couldn't resist: I read a long confession of obsessive love from another man who had previously lived in this house but had long since left town. I couldn't imagine how the letter had come to be stuck to the back of the picture, or why it was there.

"I hope someone will send this," it closed. "I am not brave enough to accept my passion."

Later that day I mailed the letter. Sometimes I want my presence in a house to have an effect beyond that of a well-mopped floor.

The Intimate Lives of Houses

I'm always on the lookout for dust in secret places where I haven't looked before to see if some has landed there. If I see it, I can't stop thinking about it until I get rid of it.
—Isabella Rossellini

I know the floors of many homes intimately—more so than the people who walk them daily. The floors are the flesh of the home, the exposed skin. Pulled tautly across the foundation, they take the brunt of the living, are first to expose dirt. I know which marks are dried peanut butter and which are knots in the woodwork. I know the scuffs, the divots, the chips in the linoleum. I know burns in the carpets; a dropped cigarette necessitates the careful arrangement of a chair. Hairline cracks in the bathroom tiles of the homes of near strangers are as familiar to me as the lines on my lover's face.

This preoccupation is not new. As a young girl playing with my Barbie dolls, I only wanted to set up the house. I arranged Barbie's Day-Glo cardboard furniture and carefully made her double bed, neatly folding sheets of tissue over a cigar box, placing cotton facial pads for pillows. I made sure to smooth the creases, ironing the Kleenex to make it lay flat. I placed each item in its proper position, inserting tiny plastic food onto the shelves of the Dream House fridge.

Then I had no idea what to do. I couldn't make Barbie talk, or answer the phone, or pine for Ken. For me, the game was over as soon as the house was decorated, straightened, and cleaned.

Even then I knew the story was in the house.

The naked intimacy of an empty home is itchingly enticing. The story in the objects on a bedside table is even more telling than a love letter.

A tube of K-Y jelly, crumpled and aging, forgotten and fallen behind the headboard, is an obvious clue. Other clues: self-help books with bold titles claiming answers to all marital difficulties. Dueling TV clickers, one for each side of the bed. Porn. Sex toys. Whips. Childproof canisters of sleeping pills. A Bible, its black, cracked cover always dusty, untouched from month to month, perched optimistically beside the bed. Post-its with scrawled messages: numbers, names.

Elsewhere in the house are more clues. At a gay man's house a shopping list on the counter is headed "Penis Butter." At a drug dealer's home there is every modern appliance but, pointedly, no answering machine.

Over time, I have become attuned to the emotional feeling of homes. In looking for good jobs, I am alert to a cleanness of spirit in a place. I look for a home that I am drawn to clean. Every house has a feel to it: angry, sad, cheerful, even optimistic. Sometimes the loneliness in a house can be palpable, uncomfortable. While cleaning these homes, I turn on the radio or television to fill the silent rooms with chatter.

In the calmest of deserted homes, the emptiness may connote clarity, suggest transparency or even openness. A sunny room may actually claim a sunny disposition. And in some houses there is a feeling that is not happiness, as such, but an energy that is neither draining or overwhelming.

The Japanese word *ma* suggests this kind of fullness of space. *Ma* is best described in metaphor: the area between stepping stones, the gap between musical notes, space revealed when a door is slid open. In cleaning a house with *ma*, I am part of the rightful order of things. I contribute to the continuation of the story. My presence, and the effect of my work, is like the draw of a good fireplace, effective and sure.

And when I close the door behind me, check in hand, I am refreshed.

But this is not always the case. After a hiatus of several months, one of my regulars called again. (I nicknamed this couple the Shedders, because from the evidence in the bathroom, they had to be losing fistfuls of hair on a daily basis.) With a voice full of sadness, Mr. Shedder informed me of his impending divorce. Though I had cleaned for these people for several years, I rarely saw them and hardly knew them. Still, I took the news hard. They represented an ideal: childless academics with progressive politics and soaring careers. I had dusted photos that testified to their commitment, both to each other and to a bigger picture. Snapshots lined the den. In these they were hippies, long-haired and be-jeaned, among throngs of people protesting against something. In one, dressed in fancy caps and gowns, they radiated hopefulness, and looked hungry to take on the world's problems. Pictures of each other graced the desks in their side-by-side offices.

But the next time I cleaned this house, the desks were cameo-free. The hinged frame on the bedroom dresser was empty and stark, like the square of whiteness that flashes abruptly at the end of a home movie. The husband had moved downstairs, into a spare bedroom. A yellow Post-it stuck to the wife's bedside table read, "It's all yours."

For the next few months, I could hardly bear cleaning this house. At any given time, only one of the Shedders was in residence. Still, there was evidence of the separation everywhere: a plethora of empty wine bottles when previously there had been only a few; a stack of worn, curly-edged paperbacks from the seventies, each advocating a different brand of be-here-now philosophy. A wide-screen TV. Then one week I noticed *his* shaver in *her* bathroom. The next week, the desktop photos reappeared.

Once the Shedders had reunited, I was more eager to clean their house. It is not only dirt that makes a job easy or hard.

· · ·

Some houses offer surprises. One day I arrived at the home of a man whose wife had suddenly taken ill. I didn't know what was wrong: I knew hardly anything about her, except for information I had gleaned from the house. Although I had cleaned for these people for years, I had met them only twice; once when I took the job and once, accidentally, at the supermarket. Standing by the deli counter, the woman had said hello, but I couldn't place her. I smiled and nodded. She introduced herself, then her husband. I recognized her by pairing the sportily dressed woman ordering a half pound of roast beef to the overly made-up one featured in several wedding pictures in the living room of their house. In these formal photographs, she's wearing crimson, or cerise, or teal, and beaming, as expected of the mother of the bride or groom. Judging from the multiplying mantelpiece photos, she and her husband must have recently married off about three of their children.

This house usually felt happy. I suspected that the couple actually were happy, albeit happy and chubby. It was obvious they were always watching their weight. Sugar-free candy, fat-free cookies, celery stalks head-first in water-filled glasses on the top shelf of the fridge. There were often affirmations typed out on little slips of paper and taped to the bathroom mirror: "I CAN lose weight" or "Healthy is as healthy does."

So when I arrived to find the husband, familiar to me only through photographs, puttering about the house, I knew something was amiss. I was told that his wife was in the hospital, but not why. Undaunted but full of curiosity, I cleaned. Vacuuming the master bedroom, I turned to find him behind me, holding aloft a puff of clean laundry, a florette of pastel sheets.

"Would you help me change the bed?" he asked.

I had never changed their bed. But in an instant we were on opposite sides of a massive king-size bed. Between us lay not only the stretch of the pink fitted sheet, but also a strange intimacy, as if we had some connection articulated in this very moment. It was odd to be changing bedsheets with someone's husband. Beds are very personal.

"That one goes on my side," he said. I tossed him the last of the copious pillows.

I should have known which side was his?

I tucked and smoothed.

Stories waft through every home, and sometimes they seem to float above the neighborhood like a light fog. From a woman at one house I learned of the "goings-on" at another house where I worked.

"Have you met the son?" I was asked one day.

This woman was Southern, blond, and like many of my upper-upper-class clients, X-ray thin. She fluttered about the house while I busied myself; I could never be sure she wasn't lurking behind an open door. Only occasionally was I in this home without supervision. I suspect I was not to be trusted. This woman had once grouped me in a conversation as "You people," though I don't think it was a deliberate put-down. To a genteel Southerner in her breezy summer home, I was merely part of the extensive crew of people who serviced her things and her life.

Her husband spent his time puttering in the garage and moving the boat around and around the circular driveway. He always addressed me formally in his pleasant Southern lilt—"Morning, Miz Louise"—and touched the brim of his cap, whether he was wearing one or not.

"Blond boy, good-looking," she prattled on about the son. "I wonder what he's up to. You've never met him?"

I heard her but did not respond. I was busy wiping a plastic place mat, one of about thirty that had been set before me on the kitchen table. I sprayed and wiped each one carefully, though there was really nothing to wipe off. In fact, there was rarely anything to clean in this antique-filled three-bedroom house. No hair in the sinks, no dirt ring in the tub, no soap scum in the shower. Did they bathe? No food hiding in the crevices of the sink, no bugs lurking in the corners of any of the rooms. Some weeks I vacuumed on top of old vacuum tracks: Hadn't they walked around?

Each week this belle proprietress conjured up a particular "extra" task so that both of us would feel okay about my somewhat outrageous wage. I once had to iron dish towels—dish towels!—carefully folding each into her preferred trifold arrangement. That day, I had seriously considered quitting.

Often I was asked to polish her extensive souvenir spoon collection. More than three hundred tiny spoonettes, each featuring a miniature tableaux rooting their origins as far away as Alaska and Australia. Several of these I coveted, and though I have never stolen from a job, I have sinned in my heart. I lusted after the one from some ski chalet in Switzerland; it was capped with a tiny silver filigree house.

It was while working here that I'd ponder the difference between a maid and a housecleaner. The line dividing the two jobs is often hazy. But while replacing the spoon collection in its little wooden frame, I drew up these parameters: dusting is cleaning, polishing doodads with toxic lotion is not. Still, this particular job was so easy it was hard to give up.

"You haven't met the son over there?" she asked again.

There was an edge here, an old story, perhaps a rivalry. We were talking about another old-monied family, their spread a mile further down the private road.

"What about him?" I had heard stories about a daughter; there had been a death, rumored a suicide. Maybe it was a drug overdose. But I had never heard anything about the son. Family pictures showed evidence of his existence. I continued wiping place mats. One purple set was from the 1970s and featured, of all things, pop-art mushrooms. I thought they would look great in a neon green retro apartment, but here they were simply absurd. This lady was *never* going to haul these out, but of course she still wanted them cleaned.

"What's up with the son?" I asked, hoping this came off like I really didn't care.

"Oh, nothing," she said, and then, because she knows I am a writer and that I love a good story, she added,

"I couldn't *possibly* go into it." She wanted me to beg. I couldn't bring myself to do it.

"Never met the son," I said.

I then made a saccharine compliment about the place mats, hoping she might make a gift of them.

Not a chance.

Two weeks after this encounter I arrived at the other home, the one with the mysterious son, to find an old Honda in the driveway, hood up. Ugh. I was tired and hoped to be in and out in an hour. I wasn't in the mood to dawdle or clean around people, or more likely, do some fake vacuuming. (Fake vacuuming means reading *People* magazine with the door closed and the vaccum cleaner running.)

This house was always perfectly clean. Often it hadn't been occupied from one cleaning to the next. When I first took on the job, I had spent two hours talking with the impeccably groomed owner about all aspects of cleaning. We had exchanged opinions on everything from French brooms to extension dusters, and discovered we mutually appreciated each other's particular cleaning fixations. But this Honda wasn't hers.

As I approached the front door, I heard fix-it sounds, hammering on metal, and a man's grunts. Then a chunk of something hit the floor.

"Hello?" I called into the screened door.

"Damn."

Entering, I caught sight of the wide-board antique

pine dining table covered with what looked like the insides of a car. Underneath the car carcass, I noted with relief, were sheaves of grease-swathed newspaper. A blond man, mid-thirties, thin and attractive, fingered a particularly large piece of the metal puzzle.

After introductions, I set about trying to find out the story. A trip to the pantry revealed a mound of garbage bags full of empty beer bottles ready for recycling. These explained a little something.

But there was more. A few pointed questions led me quickly to the goods. Jackpot! I found myself face-to-face with a gambler.

I won't buy a single lottery ticket for fear of losing a buck, yet I find gambling terribly attractive. Both qualities trace back to my family: I come from a tribe of gamblers. Certainly my brother's drug dealings were a gamble, and stories of my grandmother Rose put her in the dealer's position at her kitchen table, especially when my grandfather wasn't home.

Most interesting to me, however, are the stories of my father. Before I was born, my father, whom I knew only as predictable and annoyingly conservative, used to play all-night games of high-stakes poker. For ten child-free years after World War II, he and my mother lived on a Navy weapons base in the middle of the dramatic and newly cultivated Mojave Desert, during a time when both nuclear families and nuclear weapons spawned around them as prolifically as desert jackrabbits. I have been told that my father played well and won more than he lost. But who really knows? He had this deal with my mother: losses were never revealed, and she split half of whatever was won.

My father died when I was still in my teens having played nothing more dramatic than cribbage during my entire lifetime.

So my attraction to chance is always lurking, and I could tell this man, Hudson, in his family's swank summer home, was the real thing. I leaned in, dropping the vacuum wand.

"Gambling," I asked, "is what you *do*? It's your *job*?"

"Las Vegas," he blurted. "Poker. Days and nights at the table. When you're playing hard they set you up—a room, free room-service, the works. They gave me a table. I had to keep the game going. No problem. I never wanted to stop, didn't sleep. Months of it."

He was talking to me, but not looking at me, working on some metal thing in his hands. He rolled it over the dining table. I squirmed, worried about the finish.

I wanted to know details, to create a mental picture of him at the gaming table. He told me he had to wear a suit and look presentable. Vegas was sordid, I learned; robberies and rapes and spent people and more sadness than imaginable. "Old ladies who have blown their entire savings, crying on the sidewalk." I kept him talking, learned about his getting rolled after a big win, then about his eventual downfall.

"Thanksgiving. No money, no room, nothing. It was

cold. I was sick. Hungry. Once they get your money, they don't let you back at those free buffets. I called home for help." He grimaced and, for the first time, glanced at me. I grimaced back, sympathetically. I knew his mother: unwavering, tight, a lightning rod for a spine. Definitely not someone who would happily fly you home on Thanksgiving and welcome you back into the fold.

"I'll never hear the end of it," he said.

Hudson now had a beer in one hand and he wiped sweat from his forehead with the other. A stripe of grease appeared just above his eyebrows. Picking up the vacuum wand, I suddenly had a brilliant idea. Here was the perfect opportunity. I'll get him to take me to Vegas! We'd get a room, hang out, do the undercover thing. Live the whole seamy story. I'd write the book.

"Can't talk anymore," he announced, abruptly. "Gets me too hepped up. I'll take this out of your way." He gathered a batch of greasy metal into a sheet of newspaper and went outside.

There was nothing to clean in this immaculate house, except the dining table—which was, even after he took some of the mess outside, uncleanable. Elsewhere a little dust, a scatter of dead pillbugs. You could hardly tell anyone had been home, except for the full wastebasket in Hudson's room. Inside this basket was a slew of crumpled bank slips. I studied them. From what I could figure, Hudson had spent the previous day at various banks as far as fifty miles away exchanging money, Canadian to American and back. Somehow I inferred that he had made money on these deals, but I couldn't quite figure out how.

I spent the next hour pretending to clean and watching Hudson from the second-story window. I thought about seducing him. It could be dangerous, secret. No one would ever know.

But this particular day I lacked the confidence. On the way out we shared an awkward moment. Hudson wasn't sure if he should pay me, and I suspect he didn't have any money if he'd had to.

"I bill your mother monthly," I said, as I brushed past him in the narrow entryway. At this point he was fingering another car part and he didn't even say good-bye. I was leaving with his story and perhaps that made him nervous.

I went to that house one more time, but no Hudson. As I cleaned, I couldn't stop thinking about this family—the suicide, the mom with her cleaning fixations, Hudson and whether he had returned to Vegas. My need to string their story together got in the way of enjoying my work. I gave the job to a friend.

The house held too much stuff, though none of it was dirt, and luckily, none of it was mine.

When Dirty Is Clean

*Absolute cleanliness is Godliness! Then, who else but
God gave man Love that can spark mere dust to life!*
—Dr. Bronner's 18-in-1 Pure-Castile soap

There is dirty and there is *dirty.*

In sixth grade I was shown a filmstrip on hygiene. My teacher, good-hearted but simple, screened this gem of an educational tool directly before lunch. It was a "follow the fly" documentary. We witnessed the fly in its full furry glory, magnified to horror-film proportions. We followed it to a raw-sewage treatment plant, and watched it set down and gulp a huge dollop of crud through its hydraulic pump of a mouth, the surface of the sewage swamp roiling about its hairy legs. Then the little monster up and flew right over to a nearby playground and landed on an unsuspecting kid's baloney sandwich. There, it threw up.

Thirty years later I can't hear that particular ding from those sixties filmstrips without feeling nauseous. And I can't eat anything I've seen a fly land upon. If I'd married a lawyer, I'd sue that teacher for mental cruelty. As it is, even now I find it difficult to vacuum up the dead flies that gather in the corners of the houses that I clean.

Yet despite my fear and loathing of flies, I am willing and able to clean toilets.

When I encounter a particularly dirty toilet, I am heartened by the following fact: bad jobs are what make our lives amusing. No one wants to know that the pre-famous Brad Pitt worked in an office, but they are delighted to know that he once wore a chicken suit and passed out flyers for discount drumsticks.

My friend Laura, ex-cleaner and current window-washer ("Windows are less intimate"), claims her stint as the cleaner of an animal biotech lab as one of the world's worst gigs.

"Monkey spleen," she explained. "Animal offal."

"Awful," I agreed.

Actually, there are quite a few things about cleaning that are disgusting, several of which involve animals. I cleaned the home of a man who kept a free-roaming ferret. I cleaned there only once. (Take my word for it: you *really* don't want to come in contact with ferret waste.) I cleaned at a house where the cat was always sick. The first few visits I dutifully mopped up the brown, lumpy, soupy pools of fish-smelling vomit. Then I stopped and started cleaning around the offending areas.

I pretended the cat threw up after I left. Of course, I suspect the client was playing the same game, pretending that it had thrown up after *she* left.

However, I maintain that the really disgusting stuff is human-made. Dirt, dust, even mud, are bothersome but inoffensive. Cat and dog hair: time-consuming, tedious. Old food—dried up on counters, crusted onto floors, hidden behind toasters, forgotten inside cupboards—usually borders on icky. Still, human waste is the worst.

There is the invisible debris—the microscopic bits of flaky skin that fly off our bodies and enshroud us at the astounding rate of 40,000 per minute. All that invisible skin confetti has to go somewhere and someone has to pick it up. As a person who spends a great deal of time contemplating, if not fully accepting, the transitory nature of life, it seems hypocritical of me to complain of the very stuff of which a human life is made.

Yet as a cleaner, complain I must.

Tampons mummified in little cocoons of toilet paper like little, creepy voodoo dolls are bad.

Q-Tips in catalog shades like Sunset, Burnt Sienna, and L.A. Riot are *really* bad.

But the worst is nail clippings. Finding a pile of toenails on a bedside table has ruined my day more than once. The half-moons of fingernails are a shade less stomach turning, but barely. They cling to carpets and can hide stubbornly in the crevices between the grout and the tub.

A nail clipping is only endearing if it has come from the soft, sweet-smelling toe of an infant or someone with whom you have only just, and I mean minutes ago, fallen in love. Cherish the moment, because just as quickly as that clipping starts to harden and curl, your feelings will cosmically shift and you will never, *ever* want to come in contact with another piece of that person's petrified protein.

• • •

Being human is messy in so many ways, both externally and internally. There are obvious messes—messy divorces, messy relationships, messy finances—but there is also the more subtle messiness of our daily encounters. Often when I am faced with an interpersonal problem, the kind of stuff that routinely comes up with lovers—jealousy or disappointment, anger and resentment—I am apt to spit out "life is messy" as my catchall excuse. It never resolves anything and drives people nuts. My current partner says, "Don't even *try* that glib housecleaner's excuse."

But it is true, certainly. Overall, on a practical, physical plane, a life *is* a messy thing: a person is a mess waiting to happen. We briefly sojourn in these bodies, and then leave them behind for recycling or composting. A newborn baby is a future bag of bones. It's downhill from the first diaper. A veritable falling to bits, daily maintenance and simultaneous decomposing.

A number of days after my father died, a box arrived at our house. Neither I, my shell-shocked mother, nor my half-stoned brother could figure out what to do with the shards of tinkling white bones that half filled the plain, unusually shaped cardboard parcel delivered by the crematorium.

Eventually we decided to spread his ashes in a canyon near the golf course where he played every day. We walked the dry trail strewing the debris like so much birdseed. We did this surreptitiously, not sure if we were doing something illegal. As if we were littering.

• • •

There is dirty (dusty) and there is dirty (icky) and then there is dirty *dirty*. I balked when my best friend wanted me to visit a New York City gallery called the Earth Room.

"A room full of dirt," Sally explained. "You know, an insta-*la*-tion."

"I hate dirt," I said. "Why would I want to be in a completely dirty room?"

"It's sculpture."

I've cleaned houses so dirty they could qualify as art. Once I cleaned the home of a man who told me that his wife had always done the cleaning. Now divorced, he needed help. I arrived to find kitchen counters so filthy that anything set down on them was immobilized: the grime had become an organic superglue. The bathtub was alive with a green-brown film.

Because the whole house looked like a high-school science experiment, I suspected the breakup hadn't been all that recent. As I scraped through the layers of muck stratifying the fruit bins in the fridge, I felt like a geologist.

"How long have you been divorced?" I ventured, gagging from the stench of refrigerated compost.

"Almost five years."

I worked nonstop for seven hours. By quitting time, I had tackled only the kitchen and bath. I was apologetic and offered to come back to do the rest of the house.

"No, no! It's great," he said. The man seemed strangely ecstatic with the dent I had made. He was thrilled to find there was actually color in the kitchen countertops. "It looks great. So much better! I'll call you when it needs it again."

I haven't heard from him yet. But then, it's been only three years. Maybe I should advise him to apply for an arts grant and make the place into an insta-*la*-tion.

After much haranguing I was finally convinced to visit the gallery and, as advertised, found myself faced with a roomful of dirt. Actually, several rooms of dirt. An entire 3,600-square-foot apartment space buried in 250 cubic yards of dirt.

However, the dirt was not dirty. Not messy. The dirt was uniformly piled to a depth of twenty-two inches. The dirt was raked and groomed.

"Dirt in its place can be quite pleasing," I commented, shocked. "This soil does not in the least seem dirty. Someone really takes care of it," I added admiringly, and set off to find the talented cleaner.

For the past seven years, it has been Bill Dilworth's task to water, rake, turn, and weed the dirt in what is officially called the New York Earth Room. The soil, bought from a Long Island landscaping company in 1977, must stay moist and cultivated as per artist Walter De Maria's original installation. It was clear even from our first meeting that Dilworth takes his job seriously.

Tuesday is cleaning day at the Earth Room. The gallery is closed to the public and Dilworth, in workclothes and gum boots, takes to the pile with his various gardening implements in what is essentially an antigardening activity. Cleaning the dirt is no simple task. My trained eye can see the pitfalls.

"White walls," I said with the compassion of a comrade. "Watering must shake up the dust . . ."

". . . and mud," he added. "Those walls can be tough." I nodded in agreement.

Unlike the great majority of SoHo gallery workers, Bill is friendly, talkative, and without pretension. A painter and a father, he is good-looking, his features evenly composed and calm. It is clear that he loves his job. "The best job in the city," he told me, "but don't tell anyone."

And he loves the dirt. His relationship with it is nearly spiritual; he has a reverence and appreciation for the installation, for the stamina and mean longevity of the dirt. It has refused to be moved, swept away, shipped out with the trash. As we talked, I was struck, too, by the sheer force, the brute quality of it en masse. I wondered what would happen if the gallery ever decided to clear it out. Who would clean the room if the dirt needed to be removed and the room prepared for a new sculpture— and of what? Hair? Stones? The dirt looked so natural, so at home in the room; despite myself, I hoped nothing would ever replace it.

Bill and I talked about the relationship between a cleaner and his charge. Attention and care—the essence of cleaning—creates the bond between the cleaner and the space or object that is cleaned. With luck, the bond is reciprocal. As with any farmer or tender of the soil, it was clear that Bill had developed a respect and appreciation that has transformed the plateau of dirt into something akin to an altar. As I spoke with him, his love of the dirt wiped off on me. Context, I suppose, is everything.

A penchant for cleaning seems to run in Bill's family. His wife, Patty, cleans "The Broken Kilometer," another installation by the same artist at a sister gallery. Each summer, Patty spends two weeks polishing the five hundred solid brass rods that compose the work.

"With toxic cleaner?"

"Yes." He grimaced.

Bill clearly had the better job.

However, dirt cleaning has its drawbacks, too. Spring is Bill's most difficult time. While gardeners all over the city peruse seed catalogs and turn soil in preparation for spring planting, Bill's time is spent weeding, plucking, and snaring anything that starts to grow. Enclosed by glass, the warm and humid climate-controlled gallery appears eternally ready for planting. In springtime, it veritably screams for seeds.

Indeed, several visitors to the gallery have been unable to resist. On one of my now frequent trips to the gallery, Bill showed me the visitors' book. "Do you remember me?" wrote one guest in the roster. "In 1984 I sprinkled the room with grass seed and got booted out." During one visit, I watched Bill yank a crop of seedlings that arched out perfectly from the viewing entrance. "I think this guy may have struck again," he said, hardly amused.

Despite the rigors of guardianship, Bill is, on occasion,

pleasantly surprised when a little something springs up through the soft soil. Mushrooms arise from time to time, a type he has identified as "shaggy parasols." He usually eats these. Other, more dubious varieties, he tosses.

Many visitors to the gallery bemoan the lack of vegetation. "Flowers would be nice," commented a French guest. Others saw the fruitfulness of the room as is. "Dirt is good to eat" was messily printed in the guest book in what we both hoped was a child's hand. A geophagist—an eater of dirt—could knock himself out in this environment.

Some people simply can't believe what has been done with a whole floor of prime real estate: "I pay $735 a month to live in a ten-by-fifteen-foot studio and you've got dirt sitting here since 1977? What gives? Is this some form of economic justice? Because if it is, maybe I should live on the street and dump some dirt in my apartment."

I visit the Earth Room regularly, hoping that if I ever move to New York City, Bill will step aside graciously and allow me to take over his job.

"Only if I'm retiring," he told me, clearly intending to stay as long as the dirt does.

But to prove my worth, one day I begged to help him clean. After rolling up my trousers, I stepped onto the dirt as if it were rice paper, carefully and with reverence. It was soft and a little squishy (due to blend-in of peat moss) and . . . dirty. I walked around, noticing how the dirt changed from room to room. At the back of the room, away from the sun's rays, it was softer, richer, fresher. By the window it was crusty, hardened by the bright streaming sunlight and the glare bouncing off neighboring buildings.

"This is why I should wear sunscreen," I called to Bill, who at this point was watering at the other end of the gallery.

Bent from the waist, Bill sprayed the ground in direct, even strokes, crossing the floor as if he were doing laps in a pool. In knee-high gum boots and old shorts he looked like any Sunday gardener. We both laughed when we heard the shout of a passerby who had inadvertently caught the mist escaping through the opened windows.

Bill showed me the joys of splashing mud up and onto the walls. As water forcefully hit the dirt at the base of the wall, entire rainbows of mud splattered across the pristine white. Jackson Pollock couldn't have wished for a more immediate medium.

"Stop!" I couldn't bear all that mess. Dirt, everywhere! But, with finesse, Bill ran water down the walls and the offensive debris sunk back from whence it came.

"You try," he implored. I did, but really I couldn't stand it going everywhere. I preferred to water the dirt carefully, as if idly sprinkling a lawn.

"Have you ever considered using a different rake?" I asked as Bill handed me a thin, three-prong rake. "A wider one would make the job go faster."

"I don't have any need to hurry," he said. "I like being here. Besides," he added, pointing to the somewhat pathetic rake, "it came with the job."

Just as cleaning brings me into a different relationship with a house, my time on the dirt changed my relationship with the space. Instead of seeing a uniform carpet of dirt, I could now discern a variety of surfaces, hard and soft, smooth and rocky, higher and lower. Rake in hand, I had collaborated with it, made decisions—to break up clods or leave them? To pull or push? I had a new appreciation, both for Bill and for the dirt.

But I also had discovered a secret about Bill and his cleaning. I tell it here with the hope that Bill's bosses, if they ever find out, will know how absolutely lucky they are to have him—lover of tidy dirt, idolizer of order—in their employ.

Here is the secret: Due to the room partitions in the space, there is one portion of the gallery that can only be viewed if you actually walk *onto* the dirt. Of course this is strictly prohibited. As a viewer, I had always wondered about this hidden space.

Once I had asked Bill if he cleaned back there, "under the rug" so to speak. He declined to answer, but he gave me a big smile.

Now, on the dirt, I had the opportunity to check this place out. What I found amazed me. I nearly sat down with the shock of it—and I would have, if sitting down didn't mean plopping onto mud.

What was there was not anything you would ever guess. But I can tell you that it is *not* just another area of perfectly groomed soil. In this world things are often not as clean, or tidy, or neat as they appear. Even a roomful of groomed dirt may, on closer inspection, surprise you and reveal itself to be something completely different. I can't tell you what is back there, out of sight to visitors of this curious gallery, but here's a hint: A Ping-Pong ball bouncing off a table onto a carpet of dirt doesn't make a ping.

Lint-Free Living

Our house has gone past the "lived in" look. It has more a "no survivors" look. There are no bugs. The dust has choked them to death.
—Phyllis Diller's Housekeeping Hints

As a housecleaner I watch things appear. People collect stuff and shuffle it around their lives. I lift it and dust it and wish it gone. The crucial time is after Christmas, when heaps of worthless items are disseminated around the house. A purple-and-gold "Cleo-Cat-ra" salt-and-pepper shaker set is passed on to me, which I, in turn, unload on my niece.

I took a one-time job for a friend of a friend who collected those porcelain figurines advertised in the back of the Sunday newspaper supplements. Elvis and Little Bo Peep and a commemorative Olga Korbut poised on one toe, hands thrown overhead in what obviously was meant to be a gesture of great grace and joy.

As I wiped the dust off "Mickey at the Plate," I made a vow: I will never again clean for anyone who collects ceramic figurines.

There are degrees to the worthiness of things. There

are objects that help you enjoy and simplify life: vacuums, juicers, coffeemakers, hair dryers. And then there are those things that complicate and dramatize life: trash compactors, Water Piks, fancy silver-service sets that have been passed on for generations. The latter call for frequent polishing, especially in humid climates, and should be stored in the deep freeze or somewhere out of sight until we return to trading silver currency, at which point they should be melted down.

Why do otherwise rational people collect stuff? The eternal exchange of things: one set of dishes for another, 180-thread-count sheets replaced by 200-count, then 300-count. Pottery Barn catalogs flagged with Post-it notes herald the following week's arrivals. The catalogs arrive at such a rate that they, too, require maintenance: sorting and stacking and dusting.

Maybe we acquire in order to shore up our individual lives. We have our lawn mowers and our cars with personal names. Every home is chock-full of things that serve to insulate us from other people. When is the last time you borrowed sugar from your neighbor? Out of eggs? There is always a store open. Washing machines let us deal with our dirty laundry in private. If I have one of everything I'll never have to borrow yours. Maybe I'll never even have to talk with you. Odds are, I don't even know your name.

I work for a couple I call the Hoarders because they buy in bulk—and not just toilet paper and laundry soap. They have a stash of four or five bottles of extra shampoo and own piles of bath towels, more than a houseful of guests could ever use. The basement shelves are crammed with foodstuffs. There are basics, like pasta and popcorn, but also things like tinned baby corn and pineapple rings, items I can't imagine anyone being concerned about running out of. There are three huge jars of maraschino cherries, each of which cost over ten dollars, and always two twelve-packs of paper towels. (These I appreciate.) Though I haven't stolen from this house of abundance, I have borrowed. I took a box of paper clips (there were eight) with the intent of replacing it, and once I ate tuna right from a can. I sometimes take pens, slipping them into my pocket as if by accident at the end of my farewell note-leaving.

This house is occupied less than three months of the year. When I encounter homeless people sleeping on sidewalks, I have fantasies of bringing them to this vacation home for a vacation of their own, though I haven't. Yet.

My discomfort with the Hoarders comes from my basic aversion to amassing stuff. I think this comes from my father, a man who hated new things. He shopped at flea markets and garage sales. Our television came from a hotel fire sale and had a coin slot at the back. At the time of his death, new shirts hung in the closet. Never-worn socks nested in his bureau, alongside plastic-wrapped underwear. He wore the same holey sneakers for years, until my mother couldn't stand it anymore and threw them out.

Every afternoon after his golf game, my father walked

the canyons near the course collecting the balls that had sliced their way into the rough. "Perfectly good balls," he said, "and free." As a teen, I was embarrassed by him. Other fathers had nine-to-five jobs and wore suits. I never once saw my father in a suit, and don't know if he even owned one. But as I grew up and out of caring what others thought, his way of life started to make sense to me.

At each house I clean, I hold an anti-pageant, choosing which thing in the home is the most useless, the ugliest. This then becomes the mascot, the object that best signifies both the horrors of consumption and the essential personality of the occupants. Sometimes A.J. and I don't agree on the item. She has her own criteria for selection.

"Anything that is made from shells automatically wins," A.J. explained, leaning against a doorway, a vacuum cord looped around her neck. "Shells are beautiful as *shells*. That's it. They shouldn't be made into anything else. They're like prime numbers."

She held up a seagull, its beak a curve of clam shell, the wings a layer of purple mussels. It was truly horrifying, grotesque even, and yet I was not about to award it mascot status.

"Follow me," I said and headed toward the dining room. A.J. trailed, holding the seagull aloft, making small seagull squawks. "Pick me," she chirped in seagull-ese.

In the dining room I swept my arm toward a turtle made of clay, a gesture à la Carol Merrill of *Let's Make a*

Deal. The turtle held pride of place on the dining table. The thing was almost a foot long, made of brown, shiny clay, with chunky feet and beady eyes. But that wasn't the worst of it. No, this reptile carried a passenger. A figure rode on top, straddling the turtle bareback. A female. And there was more: the lovely lady was dressed in a long white gown. And she wore a veil.

It was frightening.

I couldn't imagine how it had gotten into the house— had it been a purchase? A gift? And how did it get into the world? Someone had to have made it. There was lifework out there I could not even begin to imagine.

"Turtle Bride," I ventured, "beats out Shelly Seagull."

A.J. considered, and balked, but only for a moment. "You win." Shelly Seagull was re-perched on the back of the toilet.

The house and the people who live there were known thereafter as "Turtle Bride," as in "We're doing Turtle Bride first this morning," or "I saw Mrs. Turtle Bride at the A & P."

Later that summer while I was cleaning, Shelly Seagull nosedived off the toilet. The nose broke off. I left a note: "The bird had an accident, I hope it wasn't fatal." The next week I found not a trace of the bird, not even the tiniest shell feather. Gone.

Clutter is the root of all evil. Dirt and dust are heaven-sent, and therefore somehow part of the world's natural cycle, but people's things are what get in the way of having a clean life. I will no longer clean for clutterers. Not only because it takes infinitely longer, every movement necessitating rearranging and sorting, but because people who have piles of everything everywhere make me crazy.

There are people out there with—no lie—three-foot stacks of papers on their desks, yellowed, curling, dating back decades. The dressers in these houses are covered with what looks like what you'd find in the bowels of the dryers at your local Laundromat: scratched lottery tickets, bent toothpicks in crumpled cellophane wrappers, dirty-edged packs of gum, and enough loose change to feed a parking meter for a week. The medicine cabinets hold bottles ancient enough to hail from the pre-childproof era. I've wrangled with drawers packed so tightly they never open, and I've dusted high school diplomas in plastic Kmart frames even though the inhabitants were well into their Grecian Formula years.

I can't bear it.

Are standards of cleanliness inherited, or are slobs reacting to being brought up in shipshape houses? Are neatniks responding to childhoods of chaotic clutter?

I clean for a gay man, and also for his mother. He has me come weekly, and she calls me when "the house needs it." In her humble opinion, this is about once every six months. By the time I am called, you could forge a sand castle in the bottom of the bathtub. A swipe across a baseboard yields dust thick as rabbit's fur. "She just doesn't see it," the son confessed to me with horror.

But this is America, where there is a self-help group for

everyone. Even slobs. So out I went to investigate Messies Anonymous.

"I was disgusted with myself," said Sandra Felton, a middle-aged math teacher and founder of Messies Anonymous. "I couldn't find anything. I'd have four or five boxes of Band-Aids in my home, but if my child skinned his knee I'd have to use toilet paper because I couldn't find them."

I have seen these homes. I murmured my understanding.

"I knew I had to change," she added, with dramatic desperation. "I didn't know if there were others like me and I didn't know how, but I knew there had to be another way to live."

Sandra put a notice in a local paper hoping to find others with the messiness affliction. The flagship meeting brought a dozen others out from their hovels and Messies Anonymous—M.A.—was born. (I suppose M.A. sounded inviting, even a tad elite, like people who have earned secret advanced degrees. S.A., Slobs Anonymous, would never have flown.)

Sandra wrote an article for a local paper, which ferreted out more messies. Then she began devising strategies for "coping" and dealing with her problem, using a twelve-step model of "recovery." Meanwhile, piles of mail began spawning in her letterbox. (Stacks of mail—a messy's nightmare!?) The *Messies Manual* followed, a self-published self-help book that sold so well it was snatched by a commercial publisher. Sandra has now authored a shelf of books detailing methods for messies' makeovers, several boasting circulations of up to a quarter million.

With thirty-five support groups operating in the United States as well as abroad, a quarterly newsletter, international speaking engagements (including one in Germany—who'd have thought *they'd* be messy?), panicked correspondence to answer, and regular meetings to attend, it's astounding that Sandra still has time to teach high school math, which she does full time.

"Math is organized by its very nature," she explained, noting that she could never teach English, a subject where too much is left to interpretation.

Official M.A. material includes the video *Conquering Clutter*. On tape, Sandra looks every bit the conservative schoolmarm as she humorlessly details the Mount Vernon method of taking control of one's house, a method apparently borrowed from actual housekeepers at President Washington's historic digs. The Mount Vernon style, which hardly impressed me as groundbreakingly original, dictates combing one's house in a clockwise direction. Each piece of culled mess is sorted into three bins: Throw Away, Give Away, or Store Elsewhere.

I had to wonder why M.A. elected to follow the cleaners at Mount Vernon, an abode that presumably hasn't been lived in for some time and hardly has the chance to collect such clutter staples as year-old *TV Guides* and free samples of laundry soap.

Yet, the M.A. industry extends far and wide. "Professional organizers," of which there are a registered seven hundred in this country, have developed skills and behaviors they claim will rehabilitate even the most chronic messies—but only those who really want to change. Daybooks with color-coded to-do lists help, as do lay-down-the-law rules such as "Any paper dated before 1984 goes." Organizers, whose ultimate goal is to retrain messy minds, charge anywhere from $25 an hour to $1,000 a day.

"A single messy may have fifty stacks of paper in her living room, each of which would take ten hours to sort," Sandra explained. "Yet they believe sorting all of it would only take an hour or two. They tend to be anxious, even paranoid, and may think you are tricking them into throwing things away. It takes a lot of creativity to work with these people."

My plans for yet another career fade: I pictured a hoarder clawing at me as I tried to eighty-six a stash of vintage grocery coupons and an abandoned, circa 1971 half-crocheted neon purple potholder.

Talking with a self-avowed messy like Sandra seemed like getting up close and personal with the enemy. I attempted to hide my judgmental attitude under journalistic interest and found myself asking all kinds of questions about what makes her, and those like her, live the way they do. Messies, Sandra shorthanded, are creative folks with the big picture in mind.

"Spontaneous, spiritual, thinking people who can't imagine the importance of dusting table legs."

My hackles sprouted. *I'm* creative, spiritual, and sensitive, and yet, at times, dusting table legs *is* paramount. (Especially turned table legs.) All of this reminded me of that tired "creativity equals craziness" equation, the one that posits that all true artists are depressed and addicted to something more dangerous than the smell of Windex. I maintain that you can be simultaneously creative *and* compulsive. I have to.

There's been a smattering of research on the cause of chronic messiness, most of which, Sandra claimed, pointed only to natural reasons: heredity, some sort of left-brain dominance, and something mysterious and, to me, incomprehensible about hand-folding in early life, something that had nothing to do with laundry. "They—we— are wired differently," explained Sandra, carefully including her rehabilitated self.

"Perfectionists who don't like making mistakes," Sandra continued. "Sentimental people who can't make decisions about what to keep and what to toss. Princesses who find themselves in a Cinderella role, who can't figure out how they got there and don't understand why they should clean up after themselves. And people who feel owning lots of things will help them to control their lives. In the end, they are controlled by the stuff."

I have often thought of my own cleaning obsession as a way to forge order out of chaos, a way to eradicate dirt from even a tiny plot of this messy world, so I was struck by Sandra's assertion that messies share the same MO as we neatniks.

"Oh yes," she assured me, "both ways of living are simply attempts at controlling life."

But I was not assured. I don't want to sit in the same (probably messy) boat as these people.

Even the thought of cleaning can comfort me when I'm stressed. As I drift into the world of sparkling chrome and gleaming tile, away go the worries about my relationship or finances.

I recently lived through a period of time when sex seemed like the weirdest, most awkward thing in the world. But one day, for the sake of my relationship, I gave it a good Girl Scout go. Afterward, in the eerie half-light of late afternoon, I fell asleep in my lover's arms pondering a better way to clean a particular walk-in shower stall.

Although I resented Sandra grouping me in with those messies, I made my way to one of these meetings, nervous and yet unconvinced we had anything in common.

I tracked down a meeting while visiting my mother in Southern California, so I drove her immaculate car—no coffee cups, no crumbs, no errant scraps of paper—and parked far away from the other arriving clutterers so they wouldn't know I was a fraud. I was going undercover and, pathetically, I was afraid. How could I ever have taken on the KGB? I bemoaned my lack of courage and set forth.

The hospital-white meeting room was empty. I was on time, not early, but apparently messies also have a penchant for tardiness. The leader of the meeting, a skinny fifty-year-old woman in a coffee-spotted sweatshirt festooned with fake jewels, started the meeting with just the two of us. By the time we had chorused, in unison, the twelve steps—"We admitted that we were powerless over clutter and that our lives had become unmanageable"—nine other people had circled the table. There were eight women in the range of thirty to fifty years old (seven wearing sweat-shirts) and one sweatshirted man, bald, about forty-five, who later admitted to having held twenty-five jobs in less than twenty years.

The woman next to me, a bouffant blonde in a double-breasted suit, turned out to be a Realtor. It was her first meeting, and she came weighted down as if she were going on a week-long vacation. She dumped her stuffed briefcase and arranged her purse, water bottle, newspaper, and bulging datebook on the table in front of her. The datebook, the size of a Duraflame log, encroached slightly in front of the large woman to her right.

"Is this yours?" the large woman asked, pointing to the offender.

There was an odd moment of dead silence. Everyone around the table stared. It was as if someone had brought a bottle of Jack Daniel's to an A.A. meeting.

"It's on my side."

The Realtor chuckled, hollowly. The datebook was lassoed. A collective sigh of relief rose up from the others. Then I noticed that her paper and water bottle had crossed the line into *my* space. Did my undercover assignment require that I, too, complain about her sprawl? I held myself back.

I took copious notes during the next hour, which I

thought would have blown my cover, but no, everyone took notes. As people shared stories of recovery ("With the help of my daughter, I cleaned my bathroom. I threw out ten bags of old cosmetics!") and addiction ("At work I filled up both my desks, so I stopped going to the office"), scraps of paper piled up on the table like crumpled candy wrappers. What were they writing? I scribed verbatim:

"I'm forty years old and my mother no longer cares if I clean my room, so why can't I?"

"I asked God to help me clean."

"It's not junk if it gives me love and good feelings."

"Talk radio is my clutter of choice."

"Whenever I can't find my bankbook, I open a new account. I have thirty."

"It's not about finding my keys, it's about finding myself."

That was pushing it. I snorted, covering my guffaw with a hand.

Toward the end of the hour we were told to define our goal for the week. A curmudgeonly, gray-haired woman vowed to use TV commercial time to unearth her living room. A woman wearing a New Agey purple sweatshirt wanted to "drink more water, an outward expression of my self-love."

As my turn approached, I got drymouth. What would I admit to? I thought of the walls in my office, shingled with yellow Post-its.

"I'll condense my Post-its." I had no intention of doing this. My plethora of Post-its attested to my creativity:

each contains a seed, an idea, scrawled or printed tidily, depending on time and place of origin. The thought then crossed my mind: I actually *am* one of these people. Worse was the thought that perhaps they too were lying and had no intention of fulfilling their weekly goal. We were all a bunch of losers . . .

Saved from my uncomfortable soul-searching by a call to rise and join hands, the group began to recite something called a Code of Anonymity: "Who you see here, what you hear here, let it stay here." Oh, well, I thought, quietly refraining from making any promises.

After the meeting, the Realtor began flirting with the bald guy, setting a date to help him clean his garage. (This might possibly qualify as the longest first date on record.) I was about to escape out the door when someone touched my shoulder. I turned to find the bank-account hoarder smiling at me. "Keep coming back, this program works!"

"Sure it does," I said, clutching my Post-its.

A Good Mop Is Hard to Find

Kerosene removes scum from fixtures,
including the outside of the toilet bowl.
— Heloise's Housekeeping Hints

I spent almost as much on my vacuum cleaner as I did on my car. That tells you something about my car and a lot about my vacuum.

It's a sleek German machine, egglike and space-age in appearance. Light and pleasing, it has features that can make or break your day: a cord that springs back into the body at the push of a button, a swivel on the hose so you don't have to fight a tangle of pleated plastic at every turn. While considering this vacuum cleaner, and saving for it, I did research. I read up, and then called the company spokesperson. I questioned him about the warranty; he told me his grandmother once cleaned for Gypsy Rose Lee and quit when Gypsy's pet monkey "tried to rape her." This clinched it: I was ready to buy.

I bought the vacuum on my birthday as an expensive present for myself. As I fanned out the stack of hundred dollar bills on the counter, I congratulated myself for being so practical. At my age, people indulge themselves with

Caribbean cruises and face-lifts, not super-sucking house-keeping helpers. "Vacuum suction or liposuction," my brother commented when I told him how I had spent the money he had sent as a present, "it's an interesting choice."

I left the store with a white, shiny midlist model. Happy with my purchase, I nevertheless glanced back at the top-of-the-line machine before I left. Emerald green. Heftier than the one I held. With a power-head that itself cost a month's rent. I lusted. Then wavered. Then panicked. Eventually, I forced myself to load the one I had bought into my rusting hatchback, but not before figuring out how many hours I would have to clean to pay for the better one.

Too many.

Instead, I gave a list of products to several clients—cleanser, my favorite all-purpose product, the preferred brand of window spray—and I included this Mercedes of the vacuum world in my request. Two of my clients are so wealthy, or so willing to please, that they bought them.

Cleaning gives me a lot of time to think, though I can't say I always ponder important issues. One day I spent hours estimating the amount of loose change thrown out in vacuum bags on a typical day. Another time I made a scientific hypothesis (and then set up a cruel experiment) in an attempt to figure out how long an ant moving at top speed can outrun a vacuum on low speed. Many days I've questioned why there's no space for a vacuum cleaner between the toilet and the wall.

(Is it because men like women on their knees?)

But this is what I've most often wondered: Why isn't there a mop that does something more than push dirt from one place to another?

Dustbusters are a bust. They're weak, ineffectual charlatans of the cleaning world. We've put a man on the moon, yet we've developed few useful cleaning implements.

Effective or not, I've found that the cleaning products we do have contain clues to American values. The "fight" against dirt is fought with S.O.S. scouring pads: the acronym represents the militaristic battle cry "Save Our Saucepans!" In the postwar fifties, when having a man about the house was paramount, Mr. Clean sprang forth to rescue women from "grease and grime." (Actually, Mr. Clean's first name is "Veritably," and despite this odd moniker, his bald head, and shiny gold earrings, he was apparently never meant to be confused with a member of the Village People.)

In the sixties, when a good percentage of America's youth went back to nature, Freewax was launched. A floor-mopping liquid, Freewax contained insecticide and promised sparkling, hygienic roach-free floors.

I appreciate a good, sound cleaning product as the ideal partner for difficult cleaning tasks. A killer spray is like tennis with a better player: your game is automatically improved. I have my own ideas about what's good, but I appreciate many cleaning products and assess them in various ways. I note the touch and slickness of a product and, of course, its smell. After a long day of cleaning, even my strongest perfume isn't going to drown out the residue of whatever products I have used.

Martha Stewart advocates making disinfectant from thyme and water, homemade scouring powder from baking soda and pulverized rose petals. But I'll bet you a bottle of Clorox she never cleans up after herself.

Still, there is ample room for improvement in the world of cleaning accoutrements. Eventually my back will give out and I'll have to stop cleaning, at which time I am planning to launch the Louise Rafkin Signature Line of cleaning products and accessories, inspired by my own intimate knowledge of the needs of the typical dirt-weary, but cleaning-wary, American consumer.

How about a Self-Cleaning Refrigerator? Equipped with a bar-code reader, this fridge would automatically date each item stored within. A continual printout would keep tabs on half-eaten cans of tuna and leftover pizza. Whoosh! A vacuum hose would drop down from the freezer section and obliterate the offender. Well-intended vegetables and fruits (which never seem as appealing away from the colorful backdrop of other produce) would be set on a slow-moving conveyer belt. After a week of shuttling back and forth, tempting but always losing out to Pop-Tarts or leftover Chinese takeout, they would automatically be dumped out a chute directly connected to the garden's compost bin. People would buy this appliance in less time than it takes to sniff a milk carton.

Over the years, I've given a lot of thought to the gender

disparity in cleaning, and to this end I'd develop a line of "manly" products packaged in brown, black, or Ralph Lauren earth-tone colors. Official studies show that despite a quarter century of feminism, it is still an event worthy of a parade when a heterosexual man wipes a kitchen counter or cleans a toilet. (A statistic: The average woman spends close to five times as much time in her lifetime cleaning than a man does.) With Tommy Lee Jones, Jack Nicholson, or Tiger Woods fronting an ad campaign for these wood-and-musk-scented products, perhaps men could be inspired to clean as confirmation of their masculinity. We can't seem to get them to do it any other way.

The slogan for this line? JUST DUST IT.

I'd develop another line of products that would target the New Age market. Scented with patchouli and incense, these products could promise "karma cleansing" and offer spiritual rewards. Each purified and blessed bottle could feature a list of suggestions for particular karmic problems, noting that the most troublesome jobs would absorb the most troublesome karma: "For maximum results, use this product for toilet cleaning." Shirley MacLaine could be spokesperson. "Consumed by jealousy? 'Envy-Away' is perfect on tub rings and obliterates any dirt or damage ringing your own aura." People are desperate for ways to absolve their difficult feelings. I say: Do it with cleaning.

Finally, although I adore my vacuum cleaner, I do think it could be improved upon. The Louise Rafkin Vacuum Cleaner would be a top-of-the-line horsepower-heavy machine with built-in radio, tape player, earphones, drink caddy, odometer, and, of course, calorie counter. If they can build exercise equipment to provide readouts of everything but your arrest record, they ought to be able to do something with a vacuum cleaner.

I once cleaned a huge multimillion-dollar beach house that was practically buried in sand. While being pestered by two annoying dachshunds, A.J. and I worked almost eight hours, filling two vacuum bags.

This particular job had been arranged and paid for by a friend of the owner as a gift, because the lady of the house had tripped over one of the dachshunds and broken an arm. The broken arm was ostensibly the reason our services had been procured, but from the looks of things, this woman hadn't cleaned her house for decades—long before those dachshunds were even born.

Our work was appreciated, though, and my vacuum cleaner was lauded. Her own central vacuum wheezed as if it suffered from late-stage emphysema.

"What an amazing vacuum!" the woman marveled, while inspecting the cracks between the floorboards, few of which had previously been visible. "You girls work wonders." I could tell we were being sized up for future use, and it made me nervous. This was not a job I coveted. On nearly every wall there were original paintings by artists I had only seen in museums. I imagined the brouhaha that would ensue if I dusted a Motherwell with a Pledge-soaked rag and mistakenly smeared the lines. I could do without this job.

"Look," she said, pointing outside to where a bevy of men scuttled around a big cement hole. "My new fishpond is going in!"

I looked. I nodded. I dusted a shelf of books that at first glance I thought were about Black Power. She and her husband didn't seem like Black Power people, so I looked more closely at the spines. They were books on black *powder*, a substance used in gun making. They were books on how to make guns.

"Perhaps you'd be interested in cleaning here regularly?" she added, suggestively. Her husband, who had barely acknowledged us, had spent the day listening to Greenwich Mean Time trying to get the time correct to the second on each of the hundred or so clocks he had stationed around the house. I wondered what would happen if I were ever late to this job.

"Maybe," I replied. "But we don't come cheap." She waved away my warning with her broken arm, as if my words were a fly buzzing her ear.

Then I quoted her a price. She paused.

"I have paid quite a bit *less* in the past."

"That's fine," I said, genuinely relieved. "I actually have enough work."

But she didn't leave the room. Sensing her wheels turning, I busied myself dusting the baseboards.

"What about house painting?" she asked. "I really don't think the whole house needs a cleaning every week, but maybe you could clean here and there, and then do a little touch-up painting?"

Here and just where? I wondered. I knew this was the type of woman who would somehow get me to do the whole job and only pay for half. "I don't paint," I told her, as I tried to abort the contents of the second vacuum bag into the trashcan. (The bags are expensive, so sometimes I reuse them.) I gave her the name of a friend, a reputable painter.

She left the room and I figured that was the end of it. But no. She came back.

"How about weeding?" she asked gleefully and confidently, as if I would certainly agree to this. "You could expand your horizons!"

"I sure could," I said, gazing out at the real horizon, past the blue, whitecapped waves and bobbing sailboats. "But not by weeding."

It was then I acknowledged yet another important use for my swell vacuum. I switched it on, and any other suggestions she may have made were drowned in the din. I heard that particularly pleasing, virile vacuum pitter-pat of sand traveling up the hose.

By the time A.J. and I had finished, the pond had been filled and populated with fish that, I'd bet, individually cost more than the price I had quoted for a single cleaning. I left that woman and her insipid central vacuum system, with my own beloved machine in one hand, the hose looped comfortably across my shoulders.

Dirt Poor and Filthy Rich

. . . comparable to the punishment of Sisyphus.
—SIMONE DE BEAUVOIR, *on housecleaning*

I've had two fantasy lives: one about being a nun, the other about being rich.

When I was nine years old, I envied the high jinks of nun wannabes Hayley Mills and June Harding as they wreaked havoc in a convent run by a stern but forgiving Rosalind Russell in the comedy *The Trouble with Angels*. I desperately wanted to join such an order even though I knew this would be unlikely. My parents were nonpracticing Jews. I figured being a Christian might be the first step toward the nunnery, so I traipsed along with some Christian friends to a midwinter high Sierra retreat for young teens.

At the retreat I discovered that Accepting Jesus as My Personal Savior, "asking him into my heart," was the thing that would "save me."

"Save me from what?" I had asked after the first revival-style folksinging sermon. "You don't know?" Chrissy Thompson snipped at me while she reapplied her pearl pink lipstick. "From eternal suffering. You know, hell." She snorted. "Worse than behind the grill at Mickey D's."

(Chrissy, who was older than me, worked at McDonald's and had a fierce crush on the youth minister.)

I was Saved during an evening snowfall. Standing outside, we were encouraged to catch the glittering white flakes falling mysteriously from the sky. "Each of you is very special," the youth minister had said, his voice low and soft. "And just like you with these snowflakes, Jesus Christ wants to keep you safe in the palm of *his* hand." My fingers had lost feeling.

"But your lives are as brief as those of these snowflakes," he continued the metaphor. "And fragile." Then, suddenly, he slapped his gloved hands together.

"Where do you want to be when you melt?"

Just then being Saved seemed like a good idea when I compared it to being a wet splotch on someone's mitten.

Although I opened a little imaginary door to let Jesus into my heart, I never really got used to him living there. I decided to let go of my dreams of the nunnery. And as for my fantasy of riches, I've nearly lost hope of that, too. But working for the wealthy sometimes seems appealing. I imagine starched white aprons, scads of fresh flowers, and crystal bowls packed with waxy fruit. In this fantasy there are shenanigans among the house staff: practical jokes and secret love affairs. Celebrities telephone the house or sit poolside, sipping from frosty glasses. I circulate a tray of martinis wearing a maid's outfit designed by Mizrahi, while famous screenwriters ask me about my work. There's a secret, duplicitous language shared by the workers—winks and knowing looks that translate to "That bitch must be joking" or "Like, I'm really going to do *that*."

My closest claim to fame is that I once heard Barbra Streisand's voice on an answering machine at the precise moment I had both hands in a toilet.

My new friend Donald's claim to fame was being the ex-majordomo at millionaire Brooke Astor's weekend home on Long Island. Brooke Astor! Grande dame of New York society. Her husband left her $66 million when he died over thirty years ago.

Donald is thoroughly irreverent. Tell me, I pleaded, *everything*. Pleading wasn't necessary, he was ready to spill.

At thirty-two, after years of peddling cosmetics at Saks Fifth Avenue, Donald created a work history that allowed him to enter the world of high-class home service through the back door. His first job was a disaster. The hoity-toity, half-ambulatory widow expected Donald to provide twenty-four-hour care and nursing, but Donald simply needed one hour off to go to the gym. "Exercise here," she ordered. "Buy one of those stomach machines."

Donald kept everything in the household running smoothly, including the woman's oxygen intake. Yet, while they were in San Diego on "vacation," things went sour.

"Though it was hard to imagine," he said, "on the trip she got even *more* cranky and demanding. She was pulling my strings so often, I felt like her puppet." Their final blowout occurred in a posh condo with a panoramic view of the Pacific.

"I threw the Cadillac keys and called her a bitch. She barked at me to pick them up. 'I don't have to,' I snipped. 'I don't work for you anymore.'

"She stamped one feeble foot, shouting 'You *can't* quit on me!' I told her, 'If I stay here one more minute *you* are going over the *bal*-cony.'"

Donald packed in minutes. As the elevator descended, he heard screaming: "You can't leave me! I can't even get out of bed!"

"As far as I was concerned she could stare at the lovely blue sea and rot."

Donald landed next at the Astor weekend abode. As chief of a large staff (which often included a cook solely for the dogs), Donald's main task was to get the house ready for Miss Astor's weekly sojourns. The household was strictly formal: silver, china, and dress-for-dinner every night. Donald himself never changed out of a tux.

"Astor is a lady against whom all other ladies pale," he said. "She never came to the table without full makeup, wig, and jewels, even if she were eating off a tray in front of the TV—which was often the case."

I found the picture disturbing, actually, this overly made-up bejeweled woman watching what? *Jeopardy?* Reruns of *The Simpsons?* "Sounds surreal," I said.

"It was. *Madame,* as we called her, never touched a doorknob or a car door handle; she never handled a bath faucet or a dirty dish. If she dropped her tissue, someone was there to pick it up."

I pictured this world as a kind of theme park: Formalityland. Donald described a room lined floor-to-ceiling with felt slots for stashing the cache of silver. An entire vault was devoted to punch bowls.

"No one I know owns even one punch bowl," I said.

"Who even *serves* punch?" he quipped. "When the phone rang it was someone like Henry Kissinger or Barbara Walters or some Rockefeller."

(I could never hold such a job because I wouldn't be able to keep from chatting with these people. Barbara Walters? Sure, I'd say, I'll get Brooke in just a jif, but Barb, how about an interview with David Bowie? I need to know if he's really *with* Iman, like *with* with.)

Despite the excitement of answering the phone, and the generous pay—$1,000 a week plus room and board—the job didn't work out. Donald wanted a private life, to actually *leave* the compound at night and on his days off. The rest of the staff wed themselves to the house. For them the situation was clear: Mrs. Astor's life was their life. Even those with children living nearby communicated with them through letters and rarely left the property.

"Working for the rich is for those who can live life by proxy. I'm not one for watching someone else get dressed to go out," Donald said like a true party-boy. "You can bet I'm going out, too." That attitude didn't fly with the rest of the staff, who grew resentful. After several months, Donald was asked to leave. "Too young" was how it was put to him.

"At least I'm not dead yet," he countered.

• • •

Donald's stories made me even more curious about working for the rich. A trust-fund friend of mine set me up with an interview in New York with Rose, a ninety-five-year-old Irish maid who had worked all her adult life in the homes of America's most wealthy. Rose had worked for my friend's grandmother.

As the door opened into Rose's apartment, all lace and shining silver, polished marble, and fine china, I wondered: How did a dirt-poor Irish teenager get work in America's richest drawing rooms?

"I'm not *Irish*," she said, when I asked if she came from Dublin. "I'm *English*." Apparently my friend, who had known Rose all her life, nevertheless hadn't known Rose's true nationality.

"I heard there was no dirt in America," Rose explained. "So I took a boat to New York City. It was 1919, and London was full of smoke. But once I arrived, I saw that New York was filthy. I about got back on the boat."

Squat and slow-moving, today Rose wore a flowered turtleneck and purple sack skirt with black, utilitarian, soft-soled shoes. Her hair was a nest of white and her eyes were yellowed and rheumy, though with a birdlike sharpness. The apartment, needless to say, was spotless. Truly. The smell of furniture oil overpowered the scent from the vase of freshly cut flowers on the mahogany coffee table.

"When I had my strength, that table shone," Rose pronounced in a lilting voice.

The table was actually gleaming, see-yourself shiny.

"It's practically a mirror!" I protested, partly to flatter her, but also because it was true.

"Things are not as clean as they were in the old days," she said with authority.

The apartment looked like it was from another era, like a museum diorama labeled "Maid's Quarters." Yet there were obvious, odd gaps in the furniture.

"Several years ago, during a tight spell, I sold off some of my best furnishings," she explained, noting my observation. "I've had some difficulties."

Rose, born "poorest of the poor," had worked for the wealthiest families in America. Her employers had names like Frick, Rockefeller, and Hearst. At one time, she had taken care of Patricia Kennedy. I sat next to her on her floral sofa, slightly uncomfortable, as I often am with really old people. I felt nervous, like I might do or say something to betray my ill-breeding, like I might sneeze and not have a clean hanky at the ready.

Though it was nearly teatime, I declined a hot beverage. Rose then directed Ethna, her truly Irish home helper, to take the rest of the afternoon off. "A gem," she said of Ethna, as she left. "Does whatever I ask of her." Rose had that air of knowing that made it clear she wouldn't be easy to work for.

As a teenager with few prospects, Rose had trained as a nursery maid. Luck landed her with English royalty, one of a staff of thirty-six at the home of a real live duchess. Early on she discovered the magic equation: big house plus big staff equals small job.

"I never wanted to work in a regular household," she said, producing a scrapbook. "Too much work." Snapshots of the homes she worked in, including the Hearst summer home, a castle looming above the Long Island Sound, revealed a life lived in homes the size of city blocks. Vacation cottages had visitor wings, as well as yachts, lakes, and park-sized gardens. Staff pictures featured rows of help in starched white uniforms. How was it to work in the midst of such excess? Was she envious? Resentful?

"I had it good. Even during the Depression, I saved a little money and never worked more than four hours a day."

As a white European who had brushed royalty, Rose was sought after during the twenties and thirties, when America's upper class hit its stride and Anglo cleaners were in demand. Their English accents and perceived refinement provided wealthy American estates with a much-desired Continental flavor. Blacks were never employed in the big houses, Rose explained, and even the Irish were passed over in favor of the English. Hiring an English staff well versed in matters of class status meant everyone knew who belonged where.

The money was good and could be depended on even in bad times. Rose stayed several years at each job before moving on—and up—to a better-paying position. About money matters, she had definite ideas. "House help should be given a raise every two years, without having to ask." She recounted the one time when she was forced to "remind" her employer about this matter. "The household secretary should have kept a record and a raise should have been given automatically," she said with emotion, as if she had never forgiven this affront that was now forty years in her past.

Job negotiations were tricky for reasons other than finances. "I told Mrs. Frick, 'No, I won't sew your underwear.' I found out that rich people can be *cheap*."

"Do I know that," I agreed. I told her about my client, Loose-Change Lady, who had paid me in coins. Rose sneered.

At the William Randolph Hearst estate on Long Island, Rose's duties as a chambermaid included making beds and dusting.

"Was he a creep?" I asked, immediately wishing I had used a different, more classy word.

"Mr. Hearst was a *good* man," she said. "What the papers said about him was rubbish. He didn't smoke, he didn't drink, and he cared deeply about the education of his children. With him, I was paid well. I went to Palm Beach, and saw Yosemite."

She paused. "And I only had to dust the *tops* of the furniture. It was another man's job to take care of the legs."

Gives new meaning to the term *legman*, I thought, but refrained from saying it aloud.

"Early on, the Kennedys were nothing," she said and continued when she sensed my curiosity. "Absolute nobodys." A condescending and haughty nod accompanied this pronouncement.

Several hours into our visit, I realized that what was so distinct about Rose was her pride. Though poor, she had never adopted an affect of servitude. "The rich just had a little more of what I hadn't," she explained when I commented on her strong self-esteem.

Her last job was an eighteen-year assignment as lady-in-waiting to an old-monied millionaire (my friend's grandmother). "Each day I'd lay out fresh clothes, a suit, and several dresses to choose from, and put away the previous night's clothing. After the lady dressed I might have a little dress to press while she had her lunch. While she napped, I'd brush and air the clothes, and then lay out a dress for supper. I'd be there to fasten up her clothing and hand over gloves and a coat. Sometimes I arranged for hats to be made by Madame Vitu. And I bought the lady's corsets; ours was a particularly intimate relationship."

"It sounds quite odd to me, sort of like playing Barbie with a real-life doll," I said, immediately interested in the fate of the exotic-sounding Madame Vitu.

"There was a routine and you followed it. And there were certain things you didn't do, certain things you saw and heard and didn't say a thing about."

"Like what?"

"Things you never said a word about."

"Like . . ."

"*Things.*" This was said with finality and a look that clearly translated as "Don't ask."

But I did ask about money. Lily's last employer had died in 1970, and she was left a few thousand dollars.

"I retired," she said. "I was just daunted by dealing with another employer. At my age?"

Retirement meant living on this inheritance and a $250-a-month Social Security benefit. At the time, she explained, her walk-up apartment only ran $75 a month, so this pittance seemed like plenty. However, when her legs gave out and she was forced to move to a more expensive place, the money trickled away. Then it ran out. At this time the daughter of Rose's dead employer began to help her financially.

"But I never *asked* anyone for anything," she said, defensively. "Besides, I'd worked for fifty years in the great homes. They're gone now. It's all gone. The houses are gone and the people are dead."

Living a rich life alongside the very rich, Rose never lacked for much, until recently. True, she had the occasional boyfriend and always kept a small dog. But a nearby tabletop of framed photos featured the children she had taken care of over the last fifty years, now grown with kids of their own.

"The wars made the world smaller," she said, cutting into the slightly awkward silence. "You young people have taken over. And young people don't know how to clean. As a girl, I learned the proper way to hold a cloth and how to turn it over without raising dust."

(Is there a special trick to this? A wrist flick? I didn't dare ask.)

Sigh followed sigh as Rose scanned the room. "Now, just look at the dust."

Where?

Rose had recently hired a once-a-month housecleaner, a "black man from the islands," to do a thorough cleanup. When pressed, Rose is not actually certain where exactly he is from.

"Use the mop here, I tell him; use this spray on the furniture with elbow grease. I tell him what goes on the floor and what doesn't go on the table!"

"He's good, right?" I ask, pitying this poor guy.

"I trust him. Other people have stolen anything that wasn't nailed down," she said. "One woman took the little bit of money I left for the laundry and left my clothes to dry in the bathroom. I've handled thousands of dollars in my life and never dreamed of taking a penny."

It seemed like Rose had adopted the manners and attitudes of her employers, and why wouldn't she? They had been, after all, her family. And I suspected that Rose's attitudes about cleanliness and presentability worked somewhat like a barrier.

Anyone could have done the actual work Rose performed; that part wasn't difficult. But maintaining the personal and private while living intimately in other people's homes must have been wearing. Serving without taking on people's judgment and without seeking understanding, all the while keeping your pride and self-respect intact, is way too big a job for me.

Rose claimed she has few regrets, none important. "I traveled. I spent money like water. All told, I had a jolly time."

As I was leaving, Rose invited me to return some night for supper. A beautiful table could be laid, she assured, though she told me one rude diner had once actually picked up one of her plates and turned it over to see the make.

"Horrifying," I agreed, having done this once myself.

Not long after my visit with Rose, I was on my knees washing a floor when I started to feel resentful. The lady of this house spent more on cut flowers than I did on rent. She would walk around her house in white anklets, the thin cotton kind kindergartners wear, and she was secretly addicted to vanilla ice cream. Several times during my shift I would catch her standing behind the open freezer door spooning ice cream from her daily pint and wearing those ridiculous socks.

If the socks became soiled—a hair, a crumb, a drip of misdirected Häagen-Dazs on the pristine soles—she would strip them off and deposit them on the kitchen counter. By the end of the day there'd be three or five or eight piles of pairs slumped on the counter. My last task of the day was to run a load of these dead socks through the washer.

While I mopped the Italian tile dining room, her five-year-old son played with a dump truck smack in the middle of the floor. "Cool truck," I said, avoiding him carefully.

"I want to be a garbageman," he announced suddenly.

His mother, now arranging a bunch of swordlike gladiolas, laughed.

"I don't *think* so," she said. Then, spying me in her five-foot genuine-gold-trimmed mirror, she caught herself.

"Not that a garbageman is a bad thing to be," she added.

"Uh-huh," I mumbled and made for the bathroom.

The resentment was like a fever, spreading from belly to forehead. There in the genuine-gold-trimmed, open-to-the-room shower, the smell of ammonia became overpowering. My eyes burned. I feared fainting.

I used Rose's motto as a comforting refrain. "They only have a little more of what I haven't."

Then I raised my rate.

Dump Dancing

Almost everything I have now has already been
cast out at least once, proving that what I own is
valueless to someone.
— LARS EIGHNER, Travels with Lizbeth

I've lived most of my life in places where garbage is picked up weekly, usually by big-bellied men wearing support belts. The trash is tossed in loud, insectlike trucks, where it is munched by huge mandibles before final disposal to who knows where. While living in cities, I've discarded with abandon. Trashing was a don't-ask, don't-tell experience. The emptied cans lined the sidewalk or rolled in the gutter, until the next week's fill-and-toss.

Then I moved to a small town where I had to handle my own trash. The local dump is actually a transfer station, not a landfill, and it is landscaped with seasonal flowers and outfitted with loudspeakers. It is one of the cleanest places I know. Big band and classical music wafts over the trash. There is no odor.

At first, I found the trip to the dump pleasant. Each week, after sorting and sifting through the mess I'd made, the yawning gullet of a large dump truck ate my white, bulging plastic kitchen sack. Week after week, munching and crunching, sack upon sack. I soon became horrified at my own personal output.

Trash dumping is akin to sweeping under the rug. Bag it, toss it, and once it's out of your hands, most of us quickly forget about it. I confess, I operate under the same MO as those guys who littered the moon: out of sight, out of mind. But I always feel guilty.

To assuage my guilt, I buzz around the dump's well-swept cul-de-sac and make ritualistic deliveries to the recycling bins. There's a station for plastic bottles, a donation Dumpster for returnables, and a small shelf-lined house that shelters newspapers and cardboard from the winter weather. Colorful bins are lined up outside, ready to receive cans and glass of all persuasions.

But the best thing about the dump is the Swap Shack. This is where I do most of my shopping. Known also as the Free Shop, it is a small structure, arranged like your average thrift shop, in which everything is free. Bring your stuff, get some more. I have scavenged just about everything at the Swap Shack: kitchen stuff, clothes, furniture. There are always eight-track tapes and an endless supply of *D.A.R.E. TO KEEP OFF DRUGS* T-shirts. My first edition of *Heloise's Housekeeping Hints* came, aptly, from the dump.

Once there was an urn, mistakenly dropped off, that was later rumored to contain the ashes of a famous actor. The person who found it spread what she thought was dirt on her garden, then used the urn as a vase.

There are a bunch of us who are Swap Shack regulars,

and most of the time we are friendly to each other. I'll pull a particularly nice baby hat, and another woman will scavenge dog toys for me. We'll swap when we next see each other.

It's bargain hunting at its best, but there are interlopers. Out-of-towners who scavenge our dump when they should be at theirs. I can tell them by their license plates and lack of a local dump sticker. There's one man, an older Paul Newman lookalike, who owns waterfront property in the next town, but he drives fifteen miles almost every day to pick over *our* junk. He's got a good eye and he's relentless. I admire him, his diligence and persistence, but if he's there when I drive up, I don't even get out of my car. There's not going to be anything left of worth. There was a day last summer when I had to elbow my way past a gaggle of New York drag queens, all fighting over one faded prom dress.

Everyone dumps, rich and poor, so the dump is the center of village life. The annual community dance takes place there, with a Matterhorn of broken beach chairs and rusting refrigerators as the backdrop. The dance is held in the fall, after most of the rich summer people have left. Families gather and set out barbecues, lawnchairs, and tailgate picnics. The band sets up at the transfer station.

One year, I held my cleaning staff party at the dump dance. It seemed apt. I invited my coworkers, the vacuumers who had nicknamed themselves Vicki Vacuum, Vinnie Vacuum, and Viva la Vacuum (this last one is French), along with A.J.

(Vicki's claim to cleaning fame is that she once sold vacuums door-to-door. Her pitch included shrink-wrapping a ham as a way to demonstrate the sucking power of the vacuum. Though she never did sell a single vacuum, she once shrink-wrapped herself.)

While the band blared country and western and old Stones' songs through the creaky speaker system, the five of us danced, ate Chinese takeout, drank beer, and gossiped. There were about two hundred people at the dump, kids and couples, old, young, all kinds. Vinnie spotted a client of ours, a woman whose summer house we cleaned midweek when she was in the city. She had fired us.

"It's her," Vinnie said. "It's Cheerio Lady! Let's get her!" We stopped dancing.

Vinnie, from Scotland, is an anarchist. I had heard a story about her once punching someone in a bar. I didn't know what "get her" might mean, but I wasn't up for a scene. Bad for business, and besides I'm a wimp.

"Bitch," said Viva la Vacuum in her sexy accent. "I think I'll go spill my beer on her." I grabbed Viva's arm, barely holding her back.

"Bug murderer," added A.J., now borderline drunk. A.J. had a thing about this woman, who left bug bombs in the house and fully expected us to clean up both the bugs and the residue from the highly toxic spray, not to mention removing the bomb canisters themselves. I had left a note about this once, explaining that we didn't work around toxins or poisons, but several weeks later we arrived to find another postapocalyptic bomb site.

The circumstances of our dismissal were a little less complicated, however. One day, in my haste, I left two Cheerios in the sink. I had dumped the mop bucket into the sink and had forgotten to wipe it out.

I was home, at my desk, when I received the panicked phone call.

"Did you come this week?" she asked. This was perhaps our third conversation in the five years I had cleaned her summer home. The house was rarely used except on weekends. Usually I was left money along with a note, something like: "Please do the bathrooms" (this after five years of doing the bathrooms) "and the kitchen floor" (like I wouldn't), "and tell me about any ants you find." "The week's yield," I wrote back once, leaving her a small collection of insects.

"There were two Cheerios left in the sink!?" she said. It was both an exclamation and a question.

I laughed. I actually thought she was joking. She didn't laugh.

"Okay, I'm sorry," I said, genuinely. I *was* sorry, I was sorry to be having this sorry-ass conversation with her.

"Were you *here*?"

"Of course."

This was getting ridiculous. She could tell the place had been cleaned: vacuum stripes criss-crossed the bedrooms, the place smelled like Lysol, and how else would those Cheerios have arrived in the sink if I hadn't wiped them up off the floor?

"Well," she said. "I don't understand these Cheerios in the sink."

What was to *understand*?

"Look, we have good days and not so good days, and today has definitely turned out to be the latter. I think it's time you found someone else."

"No, no!" This idea sent her spinning. "You can't quit now!" I experienced a twinge of malicious glee. Finding a trustworthy housecleaner isn't so easy, is it, Cheerio Lady?

"Okay, okay. I just wondered about these Cheerios," she said calculatedly, more calmly. "Let's hope it doesn't happen again." (Sure, I'll make that my birthday wish.)

Then I wrote an article about my experiences as a cleaner, which happened to mention the Cheerio incident. Several days after the piece came out in the newspaper (sans any identifiable reference to Cheerio Lady's true identity), she was on my answering machine asking for her key back. I was traveling when the message came in, and picked up the phone a week later to hear a now familiar hysterical voice.

"How *are* you?" she said, coating her hysteria with sweetness. "Did you get my message?"

"I was out of town. I'll put the key in the mail tomorrow."

Nothing further was said. I sent the key.

But I sent the wrong key.

"This isn't my key!" she said as soon as I picked up the phone the next time she called.

"Sorry, I've got a bundle of keys and without driving to your house" —a thirty-minute drive—"I couldn't tell which was which." Honestly, I had sorted through the pile of metal genuinely hoping her key would jump out at me. Apparently it hadn't.

"Do you have it? It's my only spare."

I couldn't take it anymore.

"If you'd stopped calling me long distance you could use the money you'd save to get another key cut."

None of this was about the sixty-eight-cent key. Cheerio Lady knew I had something on her, and instead of my feeling bad—what she thought would happen—I had made her feel bad.

Her best friend, who was actually my first client, stopped calling me soon after these exchanges.

The equation balanced: I lost two clients over two Cheerios.

When Cheerio Lady saw us at the dump dance, she slunk back to her car. The band cranked up a tangy rendition of "(I Can't Get No) Satisfaction" and the Vacuum sisters resumed dancing. A.J. sang, loud and off-key.

I felt a little funny. I hadn't really wanted her to feel bad. It was stupid to let the shadow of two Cheerios perpetuate such hurt feelings. I didn't want dirty karma because of a dirty sink. The two beers I had downed transformed into a geyser of sentimentality. I started across the dump.

"Hey," A.J. said, pulling me back. "It's *our* party."

Then Viva spun around and Vinnie put another beer in my hand. I saw Cheerio Lady and her husband driving from the dump in a new yellow Mercedes.

Several weeks earlier, I had actually found Cheerio Lady's key, and was aiming to tell her. But now I'd have to keep it a bit longer. Perhaps I'd give it to her for Christmas, hidden at the bottom of a box of Cheerios.

"You found the key?" Vinnie asked gleefully. She still longed for revenge. "Let's go to the house right now and pour ready-mix concrete in the toilets!"

I stopped her. "I'd never clean in this town again."

"Maybe not," Vinnie said, smirking, "but isn't there a cleaner relocation program?"

Can We Clean the Heavens?

Dirt will always win in the end.
—BOB ROSENTHAL, *poet and former housecleaner*

*I*t is the night of the comet, the one that only comes by every zillion years. I've seen it, a small, bright, fuzzy bit of sky, long awaited, much televised. I'm in bed, about to fall asleep, and it suddenly comes to me: a comet is just a bunch of traveling dust, circling through the universe, littering the sky. A dust bunny of infinite proportions. But zealous.

That night I dream of cleaning. It's a bad sign. I know from waitressing that once the dreams start, it's time to quit.

I dream of Lupita, the woman who cleaned my childhood home. In the dream I am trying to talk to her, and she to me, but only gibberish comes from her mouth. English words come out willy-nilly like some sort of child's word game: "Windex." "Mop & Glo." "Dash." "Boraxo." And "Comet."

I'm trying to tell her something too, but nothing comes out of my mouth. There is a rain of dust, and we are both covered in a gray layer of soot. Her skin now is lighter, but mine's darker. We laugh. The dust cloud passes and then Lupita is *gone. Someone far above me, someone I can't see but only sense, is sweeping. Then I wake up.*

When I was a child, Lupita came to clean our house every Tuesday morning at eight-thirty. For fifteen years my father ferried Lupita to our home in his red VW bug, picking her up from a tiny apartment on the other end of town. Though we lived only an hour from the Mexican border, she was the only Mexican I knew.

The few Mexicans in town at that time all lived at the northern end of our coast town, and Lupita lived there with her son, Robert, and her sister and various cousins. Now, thirty years later, my old neighborhood still isn't integrated. There are more Mexicans these days in the town itself, and some gangs, and a branch, some say, of something bad that people call the Mexican Mafia. And now there is overt racial tension in the high school where, when I attended, the Mexican kids, known as "beaners," mostly kept to themselves. Lupita's son, whom I knew or can at least say I grew up knowing, never spoke to me at school, or me to him. My football-player boyfriend and cheerleader pals hung out across campus from "Taco-Land," our name for the quad where the Mexican kids gathered.

I was five when Lupita started to work in our home. She had real (not my mom's Miss Clairol) black hair, and she was the first Mexican I had ever been physically close to. It was tediously warm in Southern California, but Lupita wore stockings the color of a flesh Crayola crayon that made her arms an entirely different shade from her legs. In the sixties she wore dresses, smocks really, printed polyester florals, but in the seventies she switched to pants.

Before entering our glaringly new three-bedroom ranch house, Lupita left her black vinyl purse and a paper bag of torpedo-shaped green peppers outside the back door. She carried a transistor radio that traveled with her from room to room, tuned low to "R-a-a-a-dio Tijuana." A steady drone of mariachi music accompanied the buzz of the Electrolux.

On Monday nights my brother and I were expected to clean our rooms, which seemed not unlike doing your hair before going to the hairdresser. "I don't pay Lupita to pick up after you," my mom explained. Now, thirty years later, as a housecleaner, I appreciate her rigidity, though I personally never would have taken on the job of cleaning up after us or, more to the point, working for my mother.

Each week Lupita changed a household of sheets, emptied and washed the fridge, and dusted and vacuumed everything, including on and under all the furniture. She dredged beach sand from the tub and showers. She cleaned under the rabbit cage but refused to go near the glass terrarium that housed my desert tortoises. Through mime, I learned that she thought the tortoises looked too much like snakes, and were therefore to be feared. Anyway, the tortoises were clean, as pets went.

Lupita worked for five hours, till half past one, and when she first started she was paid less than ten dollars for the entire job. By the late seventies she was earning thirty-five or forty dollars per shift. She worked methodically through the three bedrooms, two baths, kitchen, unlived-in living room, game room, and TV room. Halfway through the house, Lupita abandoned the Electrolux and went into the kitchen to make her own lunch, roasting her green chiles over the gas flame until their skins turned black and blistered off. She stuffed the chiles with cheese, dredged them in egg whites, and spun them into a pan of hot oil. I enjoyed this torture of the chiles, and Lupita always brought extra for me. During the short months of school-free summer, I tried to eat with her as often as possible, though as I got older I was embarrassed by her preparing food for me. I began to suspect that she might want to eat by herself, and during lunch the radio spouted what sounded like a Mexican soap opera, which she listened to attentively when I wasn't bugging her.

After finishing our house, Lupita went up the hill to the Medichis' house, miraculously ridding a four-bedroom home of the mess of kids, dogs, cats, and various birds by the time Mr. Medichi returned from his law office at 6:00 P.M. and drove her home. (The fathers were always in charge of transporting Lupita.) On Mondays I saw Lupita down the street at the Dressers' house, and on Thursday I knew from playing with the Braverman kids that she cleaned several places across the canyon. I can only now imagine what Lupita's body felt like at the end of each day or after a week of cleaning those sprawling California ranch houses. Housecleaning is bad on the knees and back, deadly to the hands. I never saw Lupita use rubber gloves, but I do remember her sweaty hairline and the black hair matted to the back of her neck.

During the years Lupita worked for us, President Nixon had chosen our town for his Western White House, and houses started pushing orange trees aside. In order to thwart the tide of illegal aliens streaming into this new golden world, a round-the-clock border guard was set up on the freeway not far from the south edge of town. This imposing structure sheltered squinty guards who scrutinized each car whether it was coming back from a Sunday drive or from deep below the border. Though we called the Mexicans who arrived in the locked trunks of cars looking for casual work "wetbacks," I didn't think of Lupita as one.

But Lupita *was* a wetback. I didn't know then but I know now that Lupita had arrived in this country in the early sixties, a single woman in her late twenties without papers. She had come to America on a tourist visa from Tijuana, and not only had she never cleaned houses before, she was from a landowning family in central Mexico, a household that employed its own servants.

And she was pregnant. Pregnant with no *esposo*. And Catholic. By the time Lupita came to work for us she had a son four years old, a year younger than me.

Lupita communicated with sighs: "Ah, Kat-y, Kat-y," she muttered whenever she passed me in the house, dropping the *th*, the middle chunk of my given name, Kathy, which I was called growing up. Lupita spoke about ten

English words, mostly in the request of cleaning products. I heard her say "Pledge" and "Windex" and "Ajax" (though it sounded more like "A-yaks"), but she always responded to my mother's string of cleaning commands with a barely audible "*Sí, sí*" and a simultaneous nod, whether she understood them or not.

Lupita adored my brother, a good-looking teenage surfer, who was already selling pot by the time I was ten. (Bucky landed in jail several times before going straight and reinventing himself at the age of thirty as a golf pro at the city course, where my father had been club champion and where one day his heart had stopped at the end of a round of nine holes.) Bucky, whom Lupita called "Boo-key," spoke more Spanish than any of us, a bonus from his dealings south of the border. Lupita enjoyed chitchatting with him. Whenever he was in trouble she would mutter his name in this curious chant while cleaning his untouched room. "Boo-key, Boo-key," she said, moving each item on the desk as if he would be back the next day to administer the white-glove treatment.

In high school, I practiced my Spanish language monologues while Lupita changed sheets. I patterned my intonation after Ricky Ricardo.

"*¡Mamá! ¿Dónde están los boletos del fútbol? ¡Cuando arregla mi cuarto, no encuentro nada!*" My poor accent made the whole line one smear. "Mom! Where are my tickets to the football game? When you clean, I can't find anything!"

Ironically, this remains the only speck of Spanish I can remember.

My mother refused to speak a word of Spanish with Lupita, insisting that to do so would allow her to avoid learning English. My mother, a teacher, is still mad at Lupita: "Even after becoming an American citizen, she didn't learn the language of her country." I think she thought this rude and somehow deliberate on Lupita's part. I have always defended Lupita's need to speak her native language, partly out of my own ineptness at languages, partly out of my need to tow the politically correct line. Perhaps my mother was right in some way; perhaps Lupita's life would have been easier if she had learned English.

Robert's learning English, however, was the brass ring on Lupita's carousel of dirty toilets. "*Por mi hijo*," she replied when I asked why it was she came to America. "For my son."

I went to see Lupita several months ago, my membership in the ranks of housecleaners bringing her increasingly to mind. My head in a toilet, I'd suddenly retrieve a memory of her, the way she actually *washed* our hairbrushes as part of her regular routine. Quoting an extra $15 for a fridge cleaning, I would recall Lupita on her knees facing our brimming icebox. Do I remember correctly—did she really take everything out *every* week, wiping the rim of the ketchup bottle before replacing the salad dressings with the labels all facing the same direction? At the end of my cleaning day, four or five hours long, taking my aching lower back off to the chiropractor, I flashed on Lupita. How did she do it? She worked nine-hour days.

The last time I had seen Lupita was nearly ten years ago at my brother's second wedding. Actually, she had been my date for this event.

Despite once having been a felon, my brother, revived as a golf pro, was marrying into the world of property and purebred dogs. My mother, aging but incredibly active, had broken her hip in a jogging accident and was mortified to be attending this upscale to-do in a wheelchair. I was slightly resentful at not being picked to be a bridesmaid. (I was, however, relieved when I saw the seven big-haired blondes in puffy Scarlett O'Hara floral gowns.) My father was long dead and I felt left out, a member of the family but not really part of the wedding party, even though the boy I had first kissed at the age of thirteen (actually it was more like he tackled me and stuck his slug of a tongue in my mouth as I tried to run from his house after having slaughtered it with eggs and shaving cream) was my brother's best man. I wouldn't know many folks at the wedding other than him. The day before the event, after the mother of the bride had backhanded her daughter for smart-mouthing her (things were fairly tense), I found out that no one had invited Lupita to the wedding.

I was appalled.

I can't know whether my motives for righting this wrong were entirely altruistic. Maybe I needed a cause, or to make a statement, or simply to have someone to hang out with. And I was pretty uncomfortable inviting her at the last nanosecond, as if the guest lists to these hundred-dollar-a-plate things were casually thrown together the night before. I called Lupita and stumbled through some Spanglish about Bucky and a wedding. She was extremely gracious, and I arranged to pick her up the following afternoon.

Besides, I said to my mother after I had promised to eat no more than half my apportioned prime rib and macaroni salad (and to forego the ham altogether), when we were kids, Lupita was known for her parties, and *everyone* was invited to her events. We owed her.

Lupita's parties usually marked one of the days of Las Posadas, a celebration that reenacted the three Wise Men trotting from house to house trying to find the baby Jesus. On each of the nine nights leading up to Christmas, there was a party at a different Mexican household, and for a time we were invited on Lupita's night. At these parties, white families arrived with presents—bottles of liquor, drugstore chocolates—eager to devour Lupita's cooking. Spread over a well-worn picnic table would be platters stacked with soft tacos, bins of *chiles rellenos*, and always a vat of sticky chicken *mole*, which I stayed away from because it didn't look anything like the Mexican food I got free from my brother when he worked at Taco Bell (the local teen hangout and thus swell employment for a moonlighting drug dealer).

At Lupita's parties there was always a piñata for the kids, a keg of beer in a laundry tub, loud music, and an obvious yet seemingly natural segregation of the races. The white folks drank and ate in the too-warm house, the

Mexicans draped themselves in overstuffed chairs on the porch, some of which were familiar as the castoffs from us or our neighbors. We kids batted at the piñata in turns, elbowing for more than our share of the Brach's hard candies and nearly worthless Mexican coins that finally eeked out of the cracked and shredded paper bull or Santa, snickering when, inevitably, the uncoordinated Skip Mason completely missed and landed on his butt. We all laughed together, as if we were really friends for more than one night a year.

These parties went on for a number of years but eventually died out. I suspect they might have ended because of money problems. Or maybe there were more parties, but without us gringos. Because, though we were invited to their fancy Mexican Christmases and Robert's birthday parties (where the cake read exotically FELIZ CUMPLEAÑOS), they were never invited to our Christmases or any of our plain and predictable American birthdays.

I picked up Lupita for Bucky's wedding in my mother's car. It was a hot day, and my pantyhose immediately stuck to the leather upholstery. I ditched them even before the ceremony. I noticed that Lupita had forsworn pantyhose altogether and that her pale blue dress made her hair look more gray than I had remembered.

In the car, I half attempted to make conversation, but by this time the familial stress had reached me, too. I was in a foul mood, not fit to be anyone's date. Lupita didn't notice, I suspect, and was pleasant. "Kat-y," she said, "Kat-y," and I didn't correct her even though everyone, even my own mother, was now calling me Louise, the middle name I started using when I entered college.

"Kat-y," Lupita murmured and clutched the most recent incarnation of the black vinyl purse. I suspected there was a transistor radio inside.

I cried at the wedding, possibly because I knew the union wouldn't last (it didn't) but probably because I felt like an alien. Lupita sat with me during the service, in the row behind the immediate family. Later, she sat next to me after we filled our plates at the buffet. We both ate little, but had no hesitation about taking advantage of the free cocktails. I have problems remembering much of the afternoon. I lost my peach-colored heels and danced with the best man, whom I began referring to at some point as my old boyfriend. I introduced Lupita to the bride's father, who was drunk, and I remember telling him she was our housecleaner. He blanched and then hiccuped.

We drank and drank and finally tooled home in my mother's car. Robert was in front of the apartment when I dropped Lupita off, and he helped his mother inside. I waved to Robert but he wasn't looking. His head was bowed, his arm already across his mother's back.

Now, ten years later, I decided to visit Lupita. I found her living in that same apartment. On the phone, I explained that I myself was now cleaning. Could I come talk with her?

Lupita said only "Kat-y, Kat-y" and put her nephew

Miguel on the line, who translated. After some confusion an appointment was made.

Leaving the stark, empty streets of my mother's neighborhood, I drove to the other end of town where, at four in the afternoon, people were dog walking, baby strolling, and porch sitting. I stood awhile in front of Lupita's quiet apartment before I finally knocked. When a skinny gray-haired woman opened the door I assumed it was her.

"*¡Hola Lupita!*" I said, sounding like some sort of badly accented Hallmark card.

Then I saw Lupita hobbling in from the bedroom. I had made the stupid white person's mistake of confusing her with Esperanza, her older sister, who really looked nothing at all like Lupita.

Lupita, I was relieved to see, looked a lot like Lupita, though she was much older and well worn. The black hair was now entirely gray, her once ample body had shrunk to a loose sack of bones. Her skin was mottled, yellowy, and surprisingly freckled.

"Diabetes," she said, sort of in English, sensing my surprise. She motioned me in and I hugged her as if I were touching a papery sand dollar. I sat on the floor at her feet. Miguel appeared from another room. The living room, no bigger than my mother's kitchen, was carpeted with brown shag. Velvet paintings hung on two walls.

"Kat-y," she said, and then, again, "Kat-y," frowning when Miguel explained about my housecleaning. Lupita asked a barrage of questions. Hadn't I been a good student? Gone to college? Been a teacher?

"*Me gusta,*" I said, trying to convince her that cleaning was something I liked doing.

"Kat-y, Kat-y." She shook her head. *Uh-uh,* that shake said, *I don't buy it.* It was the head shake of a person who had seen a lot more dirt than I have and knew the inside of a toilet bowl wasn't always pretty.

With Miguel translating, I learned about Lupita's ten brothers and sisters, five of whom had come to America. She talked about working for her aunt at Lucy's El Patio Cafe, which I remembered well for its genuine salsa and soft tacos. At Lucy's, Lupita's job was to watch her cousins' kids. But she ended up doing everything—the kids, the cleaning, as well as washing dishes—for just twenty dollars a week. To escape the never-ending work at the restaurant, she started moonlighting, cleaning for the Thompsons, then the Laws, patrons at the café, and fellow Catholics. Her reputation spread and she was soon in all our homes.

"George, David, Leen-da, Rock-y, Gee-na," she named the kids I grew up with.

"You watched them all grow up."

"*Ahora, viejo!*" Now, they're old! "Kat-y," she said again and smiled slightly. I knew she was remembering me as a sun-bleached, berry-brown kid.

I steered the conversation to her immigration.

"She came for seventy-two hours and stayed," Miguel translated.

But then Lupita cut in: "*Gracias por su padre.*" Her tone was serious.

"Yeah? What did he do?" Both of us could understand more of each other's language than we let on, especially when there was something we really wanted to communicate.

Lupita told a story I had heard before, from my mother, but in an abbreviated form and without emotion. As Lupita told it, one day in the early seventies on the way to work, a police car pulled up next to my father's car at a stoplight.

"*Mucho, mucho miedo,*" Lupita said. Much fear.

Lupita claimed she shook so hard crying and trembling after the police pulled away that the car rocked. My dad was at a loss to comfort her. Instead he took her home and took it upon himself to get her a lawyer and a green card.

My father, whom I can now hardly remember, was not known for his liberal attitudes. But from Lupita, I learned that he drove her many times to Los Angeles and Santa Ana, sometimes two hours each way, in order to get papers and eventually a green card and immigration approval for this frightened young illegal. Lupita was reverent saying his name, *Señor Rafkin.*

I sat on the carpet listening to Lupita describe a side of my father I had never seen or imagined. Her voice dropped as she spoke, and she carefully added that she had paid the lawyer herself.

Lupita insisted that she liked all the families she worked for, yet I tried to dig for dirt anyway. While talking to her, I learned that she still worked, and had even worked that very day.

"You cleaned *today?*" I was incredulous.

That morning, she'd cleaned the Masons' house, which she has done now for twenty-nine years. With her body obviously so tired and ill and broken, I couldn't imagine her being able to push a vacuum or bend over a tub. There was a swelling in my throat. I shook my head, and then caught myself.

It's about the money. The jobs now take all day and she is paid a much-needed sixty dollars. From somewhere— Social Security?—she gets $142 a month. No one paid her legally back in the pre–Zoë Baird days. Every non-politician I know still pays domestic help off the books.

I had meant to get personal with Lupita, to bond as two housecleaners. I wanted to talk about yucky jobs and prissy clients and find out secrets about the people in my squeaky-clean sixties neighborhood. I even wanted to hear that my mom difficult to work for. But Lupita was not going to clean and tell.

We come from different branches of the housecleaning family, branches that rarely intertwine. Cleaning, I am given carte blanche to observe lives I would otherwise never touch. Aside from this, my cleaning life gives me free afternoons and a healthy and often embarrassingly high hourly wage. For Lupita, cleaning was one of only a few options open to an illegal single mother. What else could she have done? Child care? Dishwashing?

My clients overpay me so they don't have to face the

contradictions and guilt of hiring someone like Lupita. It is easier to pay a nice, educated white girl than to engage someone who may be problematic, someone who reminds them of how messy the world really is.

Lupita sighed deeply, an exhausted sigh. There was a moment of silence, a dignified silence, before I decided it was time for me to leave. I couldn't ask any more of the questions I really wanted to ask: Who had taken care of Robert while she cleaned? Did she ever have a boyfriend? Did she want to return to Mexico? Did she miss her family? Did she *like* us? Did she ever talk with my father on those trips to the lawyers? These questions seemed too personal, too probing. I released them into the stifling air. I wanted only to get out, spring off the shag carpet that suddenly felt like a mass of creepy worms.

On my way out the door Lupita stopped me and urged me toward her kitchen. On the fridge, held by a magnet—and I couldn't help but remember that this was how my mother left Lupita her pay—was a picture of a heavy-set, dark, and somewhat handsome man standing with an over-permed white woman, flanked by three small kids. The scene was backed by snowy mountains, real ones, not the painted ones you get in a department store portrait shot. It was Lupita's son, Robert, now a U.S. sheriff in, of all places, Utah. He speaks perfect English, she told me, and he lives on a ranch. Lupita's son is successful, happy, earning a good living. Lupita had plans to visit him soon.

• • •

Several months ago I received a message from home: Lupita had lung cancer.

The news came at a time when I was questioning my use of toxic cleaners. I've often poured straight bleach onto a nasty shower floor, and though I am somewhat careful about ammonia, there are times when I do more than wince when cleaning fumes reach my never-had-a-cigarette lungs. The new killer products are faster and less work—a single shot of spray can whip away a quarry of mold or calcium buildup—but are they indeed killers? Like Lupita before me, I don't wear rubber gloves: they hamper my style. Did the cancer come from toxic cleaners? Has anyone done a study on the health of longtime cleaners or domestics?

I decided to call her. Once connected, neither of us could figure out what to say. It was an awkward moment in any language, and with my hemming and Spanish sputtering, nothing I said made sense. *"No comprendo,"* she said finally.

"Take precious care, Lupita," I said, pathetically, in English.

"Adios," she said and hung up.

The next morning I was cleaning the large, nearly spotless weekend home of a wealthy doctor. It took me just over an hour, and I charged my minimum: fifty bucks. Nothing seemed fair about anything, especially about Lupita. She was dying as I spritzed a perfectly clean countertop at a million-dollar home. An afternoon talk show droned in the background.

By the end of the month, Lupita was dead.

Dust to Lust:
Dirty or *Dirty*?

*A house kept to the end of display is impossible to all
but few women, and their success is dearly bought.*
—RALPH WALDO EMERSON

I once read a national survey that claimed that,
given the choice, women would rather see a man doing
dishes than dancing nude. There are no statistics for male
preferences. My own investigation into the world of sex
and housecleaning suggests that men prefer women dancing nude *while* doing dishes.

The business of "exotic" housecleaning is easy to miss
if you are looking for a cleaner by perusing the ads tacked
on the bulletin board of your local grocery store. However,
one look at the back pages of alternative weeklies will provide proof of these home services with flair. Right now, in
major cities across America, nearly naked and lingerie-clad
housecleaners are gingerly bent over the sides of dirty tubs
trying not to run their stockings or spill cleanser on their
spike heels.

In my own repertoire of housecleaning experiences, I
don't find too much that is sexy. I once had sex in the house

of a client, but it was not because the chintzy condo made me feel particularly amorous.

I was surprised at work by a new paramour and we leaped into the act with full abandon. There was a framed Hallmark card next to the bed. It read "Certain People are a Joy to Know." I made time in our haste to turn it toward the wall. I was anxious about the crescent-shaped wet spot I left on the pink polyester bedspread. Before I left, I misted the room with hairspray, the closest thing to air freshener I could find, and I turned the card back around.

Why didn't we have sex in one of the million-dollar homes? Because we had dinner there, after. Sushi and sunset and Steuben glassware.

So, in the way an average diner waitress might be curious about a hostess at a Playboy Bunny club, I set off to investigate what I hoped would be the glamorous world of naked housecleaning.

In San Francisco, I called a number listed for the "Domestic Damsel." Her ad promised she would "do the DIRTY WORK, nude or in lingerie." However, the number forwarded to a different one, and finally, when I got hold of the damsel, she informed me she had entered a different line of work. She did *not* want to chitchat about her former life, she said firmly. A kid yelled from the background: "Moooom!" and then the phone clicked, dead.

A call to "Clean it, Strip it, and Bare it!" turned out to be more friendly. In fact, Trina, who was in the process of buying the business from the current male owner, was a little *too* eager to talk with me. A former topless dancer, her skills in handling difficult men in strip clubs, both management and clients, led her to work as an exotic maid. Extremely articulate and confident, Trina had been dancing since she was fourteen and, a shock to me, was just nineteen years old. She described herself as tall and thin with short brown hair. She confessed: "I'm athletic and leggy, but I have a *teensy* bit of cellulite. Like about the size of a quarter."

Pity.

"Between unruly customers and sleazy management, women in the sex industry wind up with rotten self-esteem. After working the clubs, they can barely land a job at Burger King," she told me. "I quit dancing when my boss hired too many girls solely to create animosity between us. Now, I want to feel good *and* use my body to make money. *Real* money. I don't want to be thirty-nine and frantically scraping my tips together to get surgery."

(Thirty-nine. *My* age, I noted. Apparently, in Trina's estimation, this is the age for surgery.)

Trina aims to create a business that can support its workers both economically and emotionally. So far she has managed to attract enough work for herself and a few friends. Each worker is encouraged to set her own limits. The client is offered three services: lingerie (at $55 an hour), topless ($65), and nude ($85). I noted the spread; the difference between panties and birthday suit gave me pause. I would surely appreciate the safety of a lacy pair of tap pants when maneuvering an awkward vacuum cleaner on a steep flight of stairs, but would that comfort be worth a whole twenty bucks?

Trina admitted that men do like to see her push a vacuum; another much-requested service is that of reaching up to dust high places. As she cleans, the customers follow her from room to room, "sometimes chatting, sometimes just staring." Yet she usually doesn't have to clean very much or for very long.

Being propositioned on the job comes with the territory, but anything other than cleaning and hanging out is "extra." Her workers are encouraged to cut their own deals and, on top of their generous hourly wage, are allowed to keep the "tips" from on-the-side activities.

Occasionally Trina really does have to clean, and she revealed her pet peeve: hair. "I hate to touch anything with hair in it or on it, but give me rubber gloves and I'll go to town." I imagined how long yellow rubber gloves might accessorize a black lace teddy.

"Pubic hair is the worst," I said, trying to forge a connection between our two cleaning lives.

"Yes! And fallout from balding men," she added. "I get a lot of that. Lots of balding men."

I murmured an empathic word of support. "Yuck."

Trina then told me about a man who had one of her cleaners scrub the same kitchen table for the entire two-hour appointment.

"See, it's not *always* about sex," Trina explained. "It's about having company. And getting a woman to do something for you. Get it?"

"It makes perfect sense," I said, and sadly, it did. I clean homes so clean they hardly need cleaning, but my services are requested nevertheless.

But women don't completely corner the "exotic" cleaning market. Across town, Juan, who advertises himself as a "Handsome Latin Housecleaner," agreed with Trina on one thing, and that was about the virtues of rubber. "*Always gloves!*" he told me when I phoned to inquire whether he indeed cleaned buck naked as his ad claimed. "Chemicals are just terrible on your skin!"

Juan is a thirty-year-old bisexual nursing student who culls his clients from the local gay press. He markets himself as a real cleaner, charges a nominal $10 per hour, and insists that he really likes cleaning. But after a little nudging he admitted that it wasn't the cleaning that kept him working. Mainly, he liked to be naked.

"Naked is the best feeling in the *world*," he said with the enthusiasm of a teenager. "Like nothing else."

In El Salvador at his family home, he promised, everybody went naked. "Sisters, brothers, even my mother," he claimed.

"Really," I said, and I must have sounded skeptical.

"People in the Bible are nude," he added, and then, as if he were producing historical proof, "In paradise *everyone* is nude."

Maybe, I thought, but in *my* paradise everyone wears freely issued Prada or Armani.

Like Trina with her economic idealism, Juan also had a

political ax to wield. A self-proclaimed "nudist activist," he had actually been arrested for going naked.

"I have walked nude in the streets of Berkeley."

How best to respond to this claim? "Really," I said, stupidly. Unfortunately, this gave him permission to continue.

"Many people want to see my penis," he continued, and before I could stop him he blurted out, "dark and uncut." I was unable to comment. Juan, unflustered, continued. "A *big* penis."

After a huge pause and some fancy verbal gymnastics, I steered our conversation back on track. I found it difficult to believe he could live in San Francisco on $10 an hour. It turned out his hourly rate was a mere fraction of his take-home pay. Most clients paid $200 to watch him scrub and vacuum, more to video him working. And, of course, he had "a very special price for sex," which, he assured me, was always safe and, by his description, "clean."

We had talked for over an hour on the phone, and Juan volunteered to clean for me, free.

I was staying in one of my many sublets so I ran the idea by my roommate. It was, after all, her place. "We'll get the place really cleaned up," I said, cheerfully.

"If Juan comes, *you* go," she said.

In New York, I discovered a number of companies that provide dirty cleaners.

I walked into a trendy Lower East Side cafe ready for my rendezvous with two employees of Eve's Clean Club,

Manhattan's foremost naked housecleaning service. Loud hip-hop music accompanied the whine of a cappuccino machine; two gorgeous women sunk deep into a green ratty couch stared at me.

"It's us!" one said, and the other one smiled, white teeth bursting through full, geranium-red lips. Both leaned forward, giggling. "Yes, us!" The two Lisas: roommates, pals, and moonlighting nude cleaners.

I didn't know whom I had expected but it wasn't these two. Lisa-1 was fine-featured, thin, with a drape of thick blond hair. She had an air of academia, though librarianish glasses accentuated a true sexiness. I was surprised to discover she had a postgraduate degree from a prestigious university. She now worked managing a law firm and was considering law school.

Lisa-2 was tall, at least five ten, with a bob of dark curls and flawless skin. Her tight clothes revealed a curvy, sleek figure, and when she walked to the counter, everyone in the cafe, both men and women, watched her distinctive wiggle. She held a public relations job and was clearly the more aggressive Lisa, extremely talkative through a slight, but sexy, lisp. Together they could certainly star in any man's fantasy. However, these girls tried to tell me that they *just* cleaned.

"If I was going to do sex work," said Lisa-1 assertively, "I'd get paid more and I wouldn't bother with cleaning. This is *hard* work. Plus, all my stockings have ashy circles on the knees."

(This image sent me to thinking about my own cleaning

attire: high-top sneakers, torn T-shirts, and really baggy shorts with pockets strong enough to hold spray bottles that hang off each hip. My shorts, weighted down by cleaning sprays, ride quite low and thus have provided the inspiration for A.J. to coin the descriptive phrase "cleaner's crack.")

Most of the men the Lisas work for are middle-aged, shy white guys with reasonably clean apartments. "Lonely," said Lisa-2. "Not attractive, but not dogmeat either." They work for a "pretty okay" guy in Brooklyn who owns the business and skims $60 from the $140 charged for each of them for their two-hour shift. (Tips are theirs to keep.) And, though they complained, they finally admitted that much of their job entailed swishing around in heels and garter belts, wiping and dusting while maintaining friendly, but not *too* friendly, conversation.

It became clear as we talked that Lisa-2 occasionally let customers take liberties (with themselves) for which additional money changed hands (about fifty bucks). Lisa-1 didn't allow such activity, or if she did, she wouldn't admit to it. She seemed more hesitant about the whole endeavor, most secure when following the lead of the confident Lisa. When I asked if either were ever scared, say, when a customer really came on to them, shy Lisa replied, seriously and after much thought, "Anxious. I've felt anxious," and then gazed out the window onto the noisy street.

Both are in the game for extra income but also, interestingly, because of the power it affords them. This I understood. With a captive, desperate audience, anything is possible.

"There's an old saying," I said. "A servant is a master in disguise."

"I'll say," agreed Lisa-1, suddenly animated. "I'm not virginal, but doing this work I'm getting more comfortable with my body. When I'm cleaning, I'm actually sexy and I make the rules. I stop being self-conscious. Even holding a can of cleanser, these guys think I'm hot. Me!"

Lisa-1 then retreated back into her Marion-the-librarian composure. "But I'm not going to do it for very long," she added, now subdued. "Soon I'll be making big bucks and I'll hire naked chicks—or, better, guys—to clean my house."

"Why don't you two start *that* business?" I suggested. "I bet straight women would gladly hire naked men to clean. Since they're the ones spending so much time cleaning, I think those with the money would gladly splash out for Chippendale manservants." I could actually picture it: bachelorette parties entertained by bastions of young men with shiny, black super-sucking vacuums and other fetishistic cleaning implements.

"That's a *fantastic* idea," Lisa the PR maven agreed.

I left them figuring out the details of this new endeavor. "Buff boys with feather dusters," Lisa-2 said as I bid my farewell. "I know I could sell it."

"But we'd really make them clean," Lisa-the-demure added, earnestly.

I met others who cleaned for the sexual sport of it. Chad, a muscled and tattooed twenty-two-year-old, liked to work for older women who would dominate and humiliate him. "One woman said I wasn't good for anything except washing dishes and scrubbing floors," he said. "That was *great*."

I'd quit that client before you could say Mop & Glo.

Chad suggested that he clean my house for me. I wouldn't have to pay, but maybe, if he cleaned well, I might spank him.

The idea sounded plausible for a moment, but the connection between humiliation and cleaning was dangerous for me. Plus, I was slightly horrified that I qualified— in Chad's estimation—as an older woman. However, I did have a friend, a woman in the sex industry, who would be all too happy to get her house cleaned and could provide the necessary supervision. I gave Chad her number. I later heard that his cleaning was only passable: "He left hair in the bathroom sink so I made him do it over three times." I wondered if Chad cleaned poorly on purpose, seeking a reprimand.

One Christmas, a friend sent me a video entitled *Sexy Housekeeping*. "Thought you might pick up some tips," she wrote, "in both senses of the word." I raced home from the post office full of anticipation and amazement.

Sexy Housekeeping was amateurish soft porn, a campy production featuring three half-dressed babes cleaning the house of a skinny, nerdy guy. In skimpy T-shirts, G-strings, and, eventually, bare-breasted, they dusted, mopped, and sopped (the latter task, quite literally, when their T-shirts inevitably got wet and, of course, had to come off). Slow-motion vacuuming and bed making was accompanied by bad synthesized music. The climax of the video came (so to speak) when Daisy, after finishing the difficult job of cleaning the bathroom, hopped into the shower to cool off. (And, I noted, messed up the bathroom once again.) Credit where credit is due: several cleaning tips *were* provided, though "top to bottom" and "back and forth" were a bit overemphasized.

I called the guy who made the video. I suggested a video entitled *Sexy Home Repair* featuring good-looking construction workers, naked, doing simple fix-it projects. What's good for the gander is good for the goose, I told him.

"Honestly," I said when he asked me what I truly thought of his work, "I was disappointed. The women didn't really clean."

"It's not about cleaning," the director explained, a little miffed. "And it's not about sex, either."

"What's it about then?" I asked.

"It's just fun!" he said. "Fun!"

The thought of me, mop in hand, clad in a scanty lace merry widow does not sound fun— in fact it makes me slightly queasy. However, I did go topless once on the job, though this resulted in my being fired.

This apartment was plastered with photos of naked men. One showed a penis as long as my arm. I dusted it every week. There was a whip stand in the bedroom and hardware on the walls and a stack of *Meatmen* magazines on the back of the toilet. Yet, the house was unbelievably orderly. These guys were so anal they alphabetized their laundry products: All, Bold, Cheer, Dash, Fab.

One hot and humid day I was alone in this house, Hoovering with my earphones blasting.

I took my shirt off. I was still hot. I took off my bra. I kept vacuuming.

The next week I was told I had offended a male visitor who had poked his head in during my short tenure as a topless maid. Fired from the penis house. Which just goes to show, you don't always get what you pay for.

Sometimes you get more.

McCleaning

Pots can show malice, the patterns of linolium can leer
up at you, treachery is the other side of daliness.
—ALICE MUNROE, The Beggar Maid

I've been both curious and skeptical about the rise in corporate cleaning services. Over the last decade, people have become concerned about the legalities of hiring home help. There are those who want everything legal: taxes, insurance, bonding. And there are those who don't want to bother with an interview process. Some people want to make a single phone call and get their mess cleaned up, without knowing how or by whom. Across the nation corporate cleaning services have sprouted up to attend to these people's needs; each offers teams of uniformed, equipment-laden cleaners, faceless and nameless.

I call them McCleaners.

I had recently changed venues, temporarily moving to a different coast. I hadn't cleaned in several months. I missed it. I missed polishing bathroom mirrors. I missed wiping kitchen counters. I missed spying into other people's refrigerators. Besides, I was running out of money. And

I was sick of cleaning my own house, exhausted by the hay-stacks of dog hair.

I spotted a help wanted ad listed in a campus newspaper; it promised seven to nine dollars an hour for cleaning. "Join the Happy Maids [not their real name] family, the nation's #1 residential cleaning service with over 1,000 franchise operations throughout the US, UK, Canada, and Japan!" (The company name has been changed, slightly. Can I afford a lawsuit?)

I made my way to an industrial section of town and found the drab and utilitarian Happy Maids office. Cindy, the office manager, a long-haired, washed-out brunette, was trying hard to keep her eyes open. Seated in front of a computer, phone at her right, she looked like she might tumble narcoleptically into her monitor at any moment.

Since this was my first interview, I chatted away cheerfully, detailing my cleaning experience, letting Cindy know I knew dirt. Eventually, we bonded over sordid tales of Levolors and cat hair. "Cleaning is hard work," she warned, and it felt like she was trying to put me off the job. "We do *all* floors on hands and knees."

I nodded. "Mops simply push dirt from here to there."

I got the job.

And so, after John, the white, middle-aged franchise owner whose office door bore a sign reading GRAND POOH-BAH, gave me his blessing, I was welcomed into the Happy Maids family. I was given a Team Member handbook, a green company T-shirt, and an apron that proclaimed: WE SERVE.

"You're perfect for the job," Cindy said, all smiles at

my acceptance into the fold. I felt wary. The last time I had seen a smile like that was when I had accepted a dinner invitation to a Hare Krishna commune.

My first day on the job required me to watch several hours of instructional videos narrated by perky women in full uniform. I learned how to V-fold toilet paper and to properly groom a carpet. A properly groomed carpet, it turns out, entails parallel striping, accomplished by an up-and-back, lift-and-separate maneuver, a technique that seemed as labor intensive as needlepointing a circus tent.

I had heard of parallel vacuuming before. I once knew a guy who, after the first sleepover with a new lover, cleaned his house when he left for work as a parting gesture of goodwill. That evening, his lover said, "Sure, I noticed, but I prefer the vacuum tracks to run in the same direction." My friend laments ever having continued that tryst. "It was a sign from God," he said. "But no, I allowed myself to be tortured for another two years."

As I watched the training videos, several green-clad workers, all women of color, came through the office on their way to and from jobs. The phone rang and two women behind desks, both white, arranged bids by pitching the corporate line. "Happy Maids are a highly professional team of insured, bonded, top-flight cleaners," one assured in the same falsely cheerful voice that blared from the videos.

Head honcho John arrived in a zippy car covered with company logos. I wondered what it was like for this toned and tan yuppie to drive around in a white foreign car with the word *maid* emblazoned on the side. Probably not good for his love life. I wasn't shocked to discover that he was a bachelor.

John boomed a big rah-rah hello to all within earshot, which was essentially anyone within fifteen feet of the building, while Cindy, physically barring him from escaping into his office, immediately launched in about three employees who had called in sick. Apparently Cindy whined about this problem every Monday, when the absentee rate was highest, and she actually seemed to gloat as she tattled on her coworkers. Later I came to understand that complaining was her sole mode of communication; no one was immune from her criticism unless they were physically present.

Despite the false cheer of John's talk-show-host voice and the regular blast of the phone, the place was depressing. The green carpet was company color, though dirty and covered with lint. The stench of burned coffee wafted from a pot in the corner. The workers in the back room, washing rags and readying equipment, shuffled around like characters from *One Flew Over the Cuckoo's Nest*, hardly resembling the happy women on the video.

I'd been given papers to sign: one said I wouldn't steal the company's clients, and one delineated the pay scale. I glanced at the latter, thinking, How bad could it be? and signed.

The following day at eight in the morning I arrived in full uniform, meeting seven other Happy Maids dressed in their uniforms. Everyone was black except a married Hispanic couple and one bone-thin white woman named Betsy. Maybelle, a full-figured woman with a rhinestone-studded swinging cross around her neck, waxed poetic on a Bible scripture she had been reading that morning.

"Inspiring," she said. "To start the day with the Lord's words."

I watched her fill cleaning solution bottles at this totally great setup, a mix between a soda fountain and a chemistry experiment, with hoses and tubes and the smell of medicinal deodorizer. Happy Maids only used company cleaning supplies (which I later discovered to be weak and ineffective). Still, the idea of tile cleanser on tap made me almost buoyant.

I'd been assigned to team with Lena, a black woman about forty with a foot of swinging hair extensions and inch-long sparkling red nails. Lena had recently been awarded an official "Happy Pin" for staying with the job an entire year. This was an achievement worth more than a plastic badge, I soon learned; most employees didn't stay longer than a few months.

Lena looked a little like she had pulled the Old Maid card when she found out I would be shadowing her.

"I know how to clean," I told her.

My guarantee gleaned no response. There'd surely been others before me, white girls who thought they could clean and who quit halfway through the first day.

"Really, I'm a shit-hot cleaner. And fast," I added earnestly to underscore my point. Lena responded by warning me that the highly religious Maybelle would walk away if I swore like that in her earshot.

We shlepped our official supplies to Lena's crusty Toyota: an incredibly heavy old upright vacuum, a mini-vac (which I sneered at), and three huge tote bags of rags, cleansers, and other useless stuff. Once packed, we waited. Our first job wasn't until nine, even though our contract stipulated we had to be at work no later than eight-fifteen. "Time we don't get paid for," Lena said, sipping a free soda provided by John. "Get yourself one," she offered, but I wasn't interested in a generic cola. "You best get one, it's the only thing they gonna give you."

While traveling across town in Lena's rattling car, I studied the day's computer printouts. Each job was defined in great detail: what to do, how to do it, when to arrive, and how much money to collect. The what and how's were obvious. I saw that the first job billed out at $85.

"That ain't our pay," Lena warned. "Find the payroll number," she directed with one red nail scaling the page and one eye on the road. Although the job cost the client $85, a figure called "payroll" was listed as $65. "You get twenty percent of that payroll number. I get twenty-three percent because I'm team leader."

I calculated. For a job that billed at $85, I would get $13, before taxes. Lena would get a few more cents plus a per-mile stipend for driving. Neither of us would be paid for travel time, meeting time, or prep time.

Our other jobs billed at $130 and $95. While Lena drove, I did the numbers. For cleaning three houses, a full day's work, Lena would earn about fifty bucks, before taxes. I would make about $44.

"Uh-uh," she said. "You're still in training."

It turned out I'd get $16.50 for the day. My good mood began to wane.

Because our first job wasn't until nine, Lena traveled the backstreets snaking to a high-rise apartment near Lake Merritt in a posh section of Oakland. On our way into the building, struggling with the vacuum and two Happy Maids totes, I passed a white woman in high heels and stylish dress.

"Good morning," I said to her, but she barely muttered a response and wouldn't meet my eyes.

"She's off to work," Lena said, as if that made it okay for her to ignore me.

Although we buzzed the client to let him know we had arrived, we waited outside the apartment building another five minutes, until exactly nine. Finally, an older man in a sweatsuit appeared, escorted us to the elevator, and then into his basically clean apartment. The place was on the tenth floor, with a gorgeous panoramic view. With his soft-spoken English accent, this guy was polite in a way that only slightly concealed his condescension. Lena made small talk, reminding the man that she had cleaned there several months earlier. The man made no pretense of remembering her and quickly retreated to his office.

Having been away from cleaning for a spell, I zealously powered through the two tiny bathrooms, and set upon the living room. Lena took to the kitchen on her hands and knees. I was relieved to find that real-life Happy Maids didn't actually "groom" carpets anymore (indeed, the V-fold toilet paper was also a myth), but hand-wiped floors prevailed as a Happy Maid must.

Aside from a few choice pieces of characterless leather furniture, there wasn't much in the apartment except books, walls of them. I began swabbing the shelves with an official Happy Maids dust rag (full of holes but presprayed with the official, albeit insipid, Happy Maids dusting solution). While dusting, I stewed about my day's wages. Even if we hurried, we'd work five or six hours, at *minimum*. For $15.00, *before* taxes? I added up the company's cut: almost $250.00

In an angry daze, I dusted and wiped until my eyes finally regained focus. Marx? Lenin? Trotsky . . . ? The shelves were filled with books on Communism and labor relations. Hundreds! And there at the end of one tidy shelf, a slim volume I knew intimately. An academic book on the horrid history and present-day working conditions of American *maids*! Unbelievable! I showed it to Lena, opening right to the chapter on the exploitation of African-American maids.

"You mean us?"

"What do you think we are?"

"Happy Maids aren't really maids."

"A maid's a maid, Lena."

Lena knelt on the floor, wet rag in hand. This was clearly new information for her. I snatched the book from her hands and trotted back to the office, hesitating only momentarily to knock perfunctorily before striding in.

"You know this work?" I asked, holding up the red-and-black volume.

I couldn't tell if the man was more shocked that I was talking to him or that I actually read books.

"*You* know it?"

I figured I'd found an ally. There in my green WE SERVE apron, deodorizer in hand, I confessed that I was a writer, an ex-academic.

I don't think he believed me. He stared.

Switching tactics, I asked if he knew how much each of us would be paid for this job.

"I can imagine," he said, twisting uncomfortably in his chair.

"I don't think you can." I revealed the figures.

"Well," he said and cut his eyes back to his computer. I waited.

But there was nothing. He did not carry his half of what I had assumed would be an invigorating conversation about labor and capitalism. He did not offer to quit the service, employ us on the side, and raise hell with Happy Maids about unfair labor practices.

"I'll get out of your way," he said finally, before fleeing into another room. He spent the next half-hour huddled in the far reaches of the kitchen, practically stuffed into a pantry cupboard. While dusting his office, I discovered we were in the home of a prominent professor of anthropology.

Lena met me back in the office. "What's he doing in the kitchen?"

"Hiding from me."

He emerged only when we announced we had finished. In a gesture of either goodwill or guilt, he attempted to carry our vacuum from the elevator to the car. But I was indignant. It had been this kind of removed, liberal intellectual concern for world problems that drove me from academia. I snatched the vacuum from his hands.

As we drove to the next job I learned more about Lena and her husband, a laborer, who had recently left prison.

"I put him there," she announced, proudly. "I wasn't going to let him get away with that hitting bullshit. My husband don't mess with me because he knows I can make it on my own," she added.

Lena had other income, some sort of disability payment, which made her combined wages livable. We drove past a group of men panhandling on a street corner. "I don't give nobody nothing," Lena commented. "They can get a job just like me."

Although she likes her job, she clearly held a grudge against Happy Maids, and it wasn't only about money. It was about the "Mexicans."

"They get the good jobs, the ones where nobody's home. John won't send them anyplace where there are people," she said. "Folks don't want cleaners they can't talk to."

Many of the black women were resentful about "working up a place," cleaning really well, getting a home in good shape and therefore easier to do weekly—even to the point of receiving tips—and then losing the job to Consuela and Luis.

"The last lady I trained was fired for calling those I-900 psychics from the houses." Lena said, suddenly changing the subject. "You gonna stay?"

Our next two jobs were thirty minutes away, in Alameda, a mostly white, upscale suburb of Oakland. We got lost trying to find the first house, though Lena didn't mind since she was being paid mileage. "This is a nasty house," Lena said when we finally arrived at a huge, deserted three-bedroom Victorian.

From all clues the house was inhabited by a cat lover who was active in one of those "chant for riches" cults. There was an altar and chanting sheets and everywhere small slips of paper that read "I deserve success" and "I deserve wealth." Cat litter covered the upstairs like New Year's confetti; downstairs hundreds of cat statues were coated with veritable cat fur.

The kitchen was as big as a living room and, unfortunately, it was my turn on all fours.

The last house took under an hour. Like a hotel room, there wasn't a single personal item in view, and everything was colored beige. Did a real person live here? Nothing in the fridge. I found aspirin and frozen waffles in the freezer.

It was almost three in the afternoon by the time we

mopped our way out of that place. During the drive back to the office I ate my lunch.

"I'm going to get a new car tonight," Lena announced as we drove into the Happy Maids lot. "But I'm not going to put more than a thousand down. I don't want to get myself all tied up in money problems." Lena hadn't eaten a thing all day. I offered half my bagel.

"Can't stand them, can't even stand the sound of the word. Same with cottage cheese. Never took a bite of it. Don't eat anything I don't like the name of," she said.

The next day Lena arrived in her new used Toyota. She had put two thousand down, and her payments were higher than she could afford. "I'll just work a little harder," she said. I wondered how that would be possible.

"We, we, we, we, *we*," Edell chanted as she popped the clutch to get her car to start. "Who's John talking about? Who are *we*? He is talking about him*self*. He doesn't clean a thing, not even his *own* house." My second day out I was paired with Edell, fifty-three, spry, and angry. It turned out John routinely assigned a Happy Maid to travel the fifty minutes to his San Francisco apartment—"a pigsty" according to Edell—which he shared with three other bachelors.

At the morning staff meeting, John had instigated a few new policies, including adding an additional new duty. After each job we were to place official Happy Maids Door Hangers on the homes flanking each of our jobs. Of course we wouldn't be paid for this extra trot around the neighborhood, but if we pulled in any clients we would get the referral bonus of five dollars. "Five dollars each time they get a cleaning?" Lena had asked. No, John explained. A five-dollar *one-time* bonus.

"Think about those large apartment buildings," John had championed. "You could really do some damage."

"Damage to my *legs*," Edell had muttered under her breath.

We had also received a list of "Points to Ponder" encouraging us to stimulate more business, which, supposedly, translated into more money for us. "We are a *team*," John stressed. "Each time you talk about Happy Maids it is an opportunity to build up, or tear down, our reputation. Nothing positive can come out of negative attitude!"

The meeting ended with a whimper, but not before John warned us about the false promises of employers such as Kmart and Pic 'N' Save. "They *say* they offer benefits, but you'll never get full-time work, so you won't get those benefits. As you know, I've been looking into getting benefits for us here. And if Happy Maids grows, this might just be possible." Apparently, John had been talking about these benefits for as long as anyone could remember.

Even the non-English-speaking Happy Maids had stoically attended the meeting.

"You got to go," Edell told me. "It's required."

During the meeting, I saw that Maybelle was clearly John's darling. Edell told me Maybelle always went out alone, so she was able to earn both her 20 percent and her teammate's 23 percent of the mysterious "payroll." Going solo was the only way to earn a decent wage, and Maybelle had somehow made herself so righteous and so unpopular to work with that she always worked by herself. At the meeting Betsy had inquired as to when she might be able to go solo, and everyone had laughed at her. Apparently she was famous for never finishing a job. John had simply ignored her request.

"Let her go solo and you're not gonna see her again," Edell told me on the way to our first job. "A week later you'd be sending out a search party."

Edell and I had been assigned three houses, all within a few miles of each other. At the first, an infirm, elderly white man watched *The Price Is Right* while I snuck paper towels from his kitchen to clean up the urine that misted every surface of his bathroom. (Happy Maids did not allow the use of paper towels, I suspect because of the cost, but I wasn't going to tote around pee-soaked rags the rest of the day.) Together he and I guessed the correct price of the car on the show, though I screwed up when it came to the flimsy vacuum cleaner; I priced too low.

As we approached our second job, inside a gated community, Edell gave me the scoop. "This will be be *easy*. It's already clean. But this lady is a bit off. *Jumpy*," Edell looked at me sideways. "She had some operation and got addicted to drugs. But, you know, she's better, she told me last time, she's all better."

The place was neurotically clean. There wasn't a single item on any of the counters, not in the two bathrooms, nor in the deluxe kitchen. The woman was home and flying like a bird. Within minutes I knew how long she'd been married, the ages of her children, and when and for how long she had gone to college. I learned about her battle with prescription drugs, and about her valiant struggle to come clean. While I was trying to outrun her, scurrying from room to room, she tortured Edell, talking at her, telling her the same stories. And when neither of us could be cornered, she blathered at the cat. "Pussy, pussy, I love you," she sang like a record spinning at the wrong speed. "Pussy, pussy, lovekins, lamby-poo, *sweetypie*, you know I love you!" The cat dashed about, no doubt trying to flee from her as well.

Eventually the woman trapped me in the bathroom. I was caressing the underside of her toilet. "I must bid farewell," she said dramatically. "I hope to see you again, Lois? Laura? LeeAnn? What *was* your name?"

Before I had a chance to answer, she reached under the sink and shook a marimba of pills from an orchestra of bottles and swallowed the entire cocktail professionally—one gulp, no water. Then she left. I couldn't help myself. I peeked. Painkillers, antidepressants, Valium.

Clean? Well, the house was.

"For real?" Edell said when I told her about the pills.

Our day progressed, the only screw-up was a mix-up in the schedule. After we had dragged our equipment two flights up to a second-floor condo, Edell placed the requisite call to the office only to find out our work order had changed. We spent an hour of unpaid time repacking our stuff and driving to a different job because of a mistake made at the office. Of course, no one offered to reimburse us for our time.

That second day, I made a whopping $36, pre-tax, even at the after-training rate. I had to quit. Driving home, Edell tried to talk me into staying, but news of her $160-a-week take-home pay was hardly encouragement. Lena made $40 to $60 more than Edell, but it turned out she came to work early—at seven—and worked weekends washing and folding the Happy Maids' laundry.

I don't have much experience quitting jobs, so I actually felt nervous standing outside the Grand Poohbah's office. Edell whispered encouragement. "He's been sitting in front of that computer too long. Anybody sit in front of a computer that long *has* to be cheating someone."

"Come on in!" John bellowed. "I hear you're our new whiz kid. Sit yourself down. How's it going?"

"It went," I said. "But it's not really *going* anywhere. This isn't working out for me."

John leaned across his desk, feigning concern. "I mean, I don't know you from Adam—or maybe I should say Eve, to be politically correct—but incoming reports tell me you are doing real well."

"Not well enough," I said. "I can't clean any faster, yet I figure I'll make less than five dollars an hour. Plus I'll put all that mileage on my car. I don't see how I could ever earn the nine or even seven dollars an hour you advertised."

John seemed taken aback. He sat back in his chair. "I don't know how you worked as an independent, but everything here is above board. I'm looking at"—and here he swept his hand across his cluttered desk—"thousands of dollars in bills and taxes. Here at Happy Maids we go *totally* by the book. That costs money, lots of money."

"Someone here is making money, John," I said, my heart thumping, "but it's not the people doing the work."

The last time I had seen a face cloud over like this was when I went to buy a new car and insisted I get the deal I'd been promised over the phone.

John would have fled if he could have, but he was pinned behind the desk. I offered my hand, which he took hesitantly and shook weakly. "Well, well," he muttered as I left.

I said good-bye to Edell in the parking lot, taking her phone number and promising to call her if I found extra work. I encouraged her to put her number up at her local grocery store. She lived in Albany, in a fairly nice neighborhood; surely there were local people who needed a good cleaner.

"With only three or four jobs a week, you'd earn more than you do as a Happy Maid."

She paused and looked across the lot to where Lena was showing Maybelle her car. "Who's going to hire me? Who's going to let *me* in their house?" she asked.

And though I immediately responded, "Someone will, you're a great cleaner," I knew it was a lie.

John and his Happy Maids office staff make it okay

for rich people to allow people they are normally afraid of into their homes. People will trust nameless faces as long as they are in uniform, and as long as they know their place. A Happy Maid would always know her place; the amount of her paycheck would make her value perfectly clear.

Having It Maid

*(Useful Information for those who thought
this book was about cleaning)*

Many people complain about the lack of available good help. These are usually the same people who don't know how to treat good help.

Tips for employers:

- Don't be home.
- If you are home, know that when your house is being cleaned it is no longer yours. Many of you will hate this, I know, I can hear you—"Who does she think she is?" But think about it. You'd let a man, say a carpenter or plumber, take over and traipse through your home, even if he were wearing heavy work-boots. A good housecleaner deserves equal respect and won't scuff your floors.
- Leave a friendly, appreciative note and acknowledge extras, like "You are amazing!" And, "You oiled the furniture —wow!"

- Don't let a week's worth (or even a morning's worth) of dirty dishes pile up in the sink just because you know your cleaner is coming and will have to wade elbow deep through mounds of dishes in order to find the sink so she can then scour it.

- Leave treats and beverages. Remember: A happy cleaner will probably remove that two-inch cockroach from under the fridge. A disgruntled cleaner will simply relocate it onto the toilet seat. Note: A treat is not anything that was given to you last Christmas—like an old fruitcake. We *know* what's been hanging around.

- Apologize for dog or cat hair. Better yet, take your big scary dog with you when you know your cleaner is coming. Who wants him barking at the vacuum or trodding on the newly washed floor? Not us.

- Pick up dirty underwear and anything else even vaguely associated with bodily fluids. Wadded Kleenex is bad. Wadded and hidden in the sheets is the worst. These clumped-up bits of fluff tell a story we don't want to know. I once had a client I called the Gerbil. I assumed she had allergies. The shredded tissues papering her bed resembled the floor of a Habitrail. I walked out of another place after discovering a wad of used condoms of indeterminate age practically welded to a bedroom floor. If you won't touch it, what makes you think we will?

- Paper towels—and not cheap ones—are what housecleaners dream of on cold winter nights. Purchase these by the dozen.

- Don't ask your housecleaner to do tasks like wash and fold your grown children's camp wardrobe from 1962 just because you're afraid you're not getting your money's worth.

- Nix directions involving "extra attention" such as "pay extra attention to the grout under the toilet—anything we can do about the yellowing?" Any decent housecleaner lives firmly by my own personal motto: CLEANING, NOT RESTORATION.

- Find out who your housecleaner is. More than "from Mexico." What most employers know about their cleaners is comparable to what Alex Trebek knows about a single *Jeopardy* contestant.

- Make sure toilets are flushed. You'd be mortified to know how many people don't make this gesture—but not half as mortified as we cleaners are.

A Visit with Persephone

*Those whom you let approach the pit of blood
will speak the truth to you.*
—The Odyssey

I was once asked to clean up after a suicide. I didn't do it. I pretended I didn't get the message. Later, I found out who cleaned, and that blood is impossible to get off white walls.

I specialize in cleaning *clean* houses.

Kathy Jo Kadziauskas specializes in cleaning up after crime scenes. Murders. Suicides. And "de-comps," insider slang for dead bodies that have been laying around awhile.

As I drove the winding road to the small town north of Los Angeles where Kathy Jo lives in close proximity to five high-crime counties, I wondered what we would talk about. With cleaning buddies I love to talk about our relationships with our clients, but that wasn't possible: Kathy Jo didn't get to know her clients. The people she cleaned up after had already reached the end of the line. ("I have no repeat customers," she said later, with a sinister inflection.)

Still, cleaning *is* cleaning. Both of us worked to eradicate evidence.

An innocuous, brown wood-paneled quick-build from the seventies, Kathy Jo's apartment complex seemed shabby and sad, like one of those places where people live, sharing walls and the blare from their televisions, without learning each other's names. The inside of her apartment, however, told another story. Deco and Betty Boop figurines crowded the dusty surfaces of the dark wood tables. Silk flowers wreathed the ceiling, antique couches were veiled with fringed scarfs and gilded shawls. A good looking, well-put-together fifty-year-old with false eyelashes and a cap of copper red and blond–streaked hair, Kathy Jo is clearly, despite her profession, a romantic.

"Someone died on that one," Kathy Jo said, pointing to the wood and white-brocade couch on which I was seated. "So the client gave it to me. Luckily, I could get all the blood out."

I moved to a nearby rocker (too small to die on, I hoped) and looked around. The apartment looked like one of those over-decorated gift shops, the kind that somehow stay afloat selling only candles and Christmas decorations year-round. Still, any approximation of elegance must be refreshing after wiping brains off a chandelier.

Kathy Jo had been a salesperson before she got into the post-crime business, and this was obvious. Sensing an opportunity in the burgeoning business of after-accident cleanup, she leaped at the chance to be her own boss and has never looked back. Yet, after several years, her business isn't out of the red. This nascent service industry is highly competitive: there are now five other cleanup operations in the Los Angeles area, several of which undercut Kathy Jo's prices. The drop in the crime rate hasn't helped much either.

"People think this is an easy way to make a few bucks," she commented, in a distinct tone of I-know-this-business-best. "Just let them try it."

As I flipped through photos of Kathy Jo and her crew ripping up bloodstained carpets and hauling Hefty bags full of shredded mattress contaminated with bits of decomposed body and maggots, I puzzled: People think this is *easy*?

I had loitered for a week in Los Angeles trying to go on the job with Kathy Jo. I'd assured her that I was a good cleaner, and had flippantly promised that I wasn't the kind of woman who would throw up at the sight of a bug. But after hearing the description of maggot swarms at decomp sites, I knew I'd never be able to stomach this work. Once I arrived at a job where the occupants had gone on vacation and mistakenly left a chicken in the basement, outside the freezer. I discovered the offender, maggot-riddled and fly-flocked, a week after it had hit the air, identifiable only by its gooey supermarket label. Miraculously, I managed to get rid of the thing, bundling it into the trash can, dry-retching the entire time. I didn't even get tipped for this job; all the woman said when I told of the errant poultry was, "Oh my!"

So, gloves or no gloves, there was no way I could handle a marathon of maggots worming their way through human remains. I was outwardly disappointed but secretly relieved when it turned out to be a slow crime week. Yet a scarcity of corpses did not mean Kathy Jo had enjoyed a week's vacation. She had pulled a quick job a few days before my arrival—a single-shot suicide, called a "simple blood" in her specialized lingo. The rest of the week had been spent delivering Valentine candy to those in the position to advise survivors about her services: cops, sheriffs, and coroners.

"But there's only so much schmoozing I can do," she admitted, clearly a little edgy about not knowing when she would next don her yellow safety jumpsuit. Though her employment horizon is always hazy, tax time was approaching—and she was figuring that would bring on a spate of suicides. "Right now, I need something to happen."

On cue, the phone rang. Kathy Jo jumped for it. I feared my day might take a turn. But then she shook her head, gave me a thumb's down, and began dickering with an insurance company. Professional and courteous with the agent, Kathy Jo is one of the few in the business who deal with insurance claims. (Most homeowner policies will cover crime cleanup under "property damage," though they don't advertise this.) She showed me her intake evaluation, which helped her make claims and also quote a price over the phone. The questions seemed a little gruesome: "Caliber of gun used?" it read. I grimaced.

"A crucial question in a gun-shot cleanup," she said. "Caliber dictates how much area may need my attention."

I refrained from asking details. My own job intake questions paled. "Pets?" just didn't compare.

• • •

This is a true but nevertheless disconcerting fact: there are people living in our world hoping for the worst. ER doctors gleeful for bloody car wrecks; firefighters who cringe at false alarms; cops who dream of pulling guns on fleeing criminals. Kathy Jo is one of these disaster junkies, perhaps even more so than other professionals who get paid whether disaster strikes or not. Happy for the work, sorry for the situation, she faces suffering and sadness at every one of her job sites. Part pastor, part pal, she winds up learning about the deceased even though she would rather not. At one site the extended family of a man who shot himself in his suburban bathroom held a picnic in the backyard while her crew scraped their father/brother/husband out of the bathtub.

"It was the weirdest thing," Kathy Jo said, shaking her head. "People eating french fries and Happy Meals ten feet from this suicide site."

"I never see the whole bodies," she added. "And I don't allow the families to show me pictures. They want to, but I'd rather not hear them reminisce about Uncle George while I'm cleaning him off the floor."

Her strangest job was the autoerotic death that left her picking through remains and remembrances of a life she at first thought was simply pathetic. Homeless, the victim had hung himself in his rented storage unit; he was found in a woman's black lace bodysuit, amidst a tangle of sexual paraphernalia. Cops and coroners smirked, as did Kathy Jo and her crew. But digging deeper through the mounds of this man's stored junk, they discovered pictures of an ex-wife who had apparently also killed herself, evidence of a large family, and, most disturbing to Kathy Jo, the makings of a fully stocked kitchen packed neatly in boxes.

"Matched plates, silverware, four sizes of glasses," she said. "How had he gone from Tupperware to this? Where is the cause-and-effect in a life like this?"

Like all of us in the community of cleaners, Kathy Jo finds herself trying to make sense of too much information. "It's a disrespectful business. What I discover is much worse than finding a car-crash victim wearing dirty underwear. I arrive in the middle of the story. I know what has happened, but I don't know how life will go on for those left. Mostly I try not to let myself get involved."

Inevitably, she sometimes does get involved. She has thrown out compromising photos when she sensed they would disturb bereaved family members. I confessed to her my own experience changing "evidence" at job sites, and the lies I have heard and have become complicit with. We both talk about how intimate we are with people we don't know. But cleaning up actual bodily remains—and the creepy human story contained in DNA—seems to me beyond intimate.

I found myself, like most people Kathy Jo encounters, repulsed and then curious. I wanted to know what body remains felt like on the backside of a sponge. Soft? Or hard like a cadaver?

"Either, or both, depending on time passed and place."

Maggots . . . wipe?

"No. *Vacuum*."

And what about the smell? Kathy Jo douses with special minerals, from Australia, called, ironically, Ex-Stink. In fact, she is now the zealous North American distributor of this environmentally friendly miracle potion.

"And we're not maids, we don't do toilets," she pronounced. The crew cleans up anything touched by the body or body fluids; everything else is left as is. Apparently this can be a shock to some people who think they are coming back to a good-as-new abode and instead find bare floorboards, hacked-up furniture, and huge holes in the carpet.

"There's still a mess," she said. "One way or another."

How did she learn this craft?

"Trial and error," she admitted, steering me into her kitchen. She pointed at the cat bowl containing several partially gnawed pieces of red flesh. "Liver. It's great practice material. Put it in the blender. Essentially, there you have it."

I backed out of the kitchen, quickly.

Back in the loop-de-loop of the Los Angeles freeways, with sample packets of Ex-Stink on the seat beside me, I drove for over an hour through smog-shrouded and quite possibly crime-riddled suburbs. Maybe Kathy Jo's phone would ring soon, maybe even tonight.

I could never go in for body cleanup: hair and fingernails off live people are bad enough. The pleasure I get from cleaning depends on leaving a site better than I found it, full of possibility, offering its inhabitants a chance for a fresh start.

Kathy Jo must satisfy herself with getting rid of the worst of a bad thing.

Polishing the Big Apple

*By taking our place in the home and doing many of our
jobs, you can give us free hours to do the things we
enjoy — playing golf, sewing, playing the piano,
attending club meetings, or working at a job we like.*
—Your Maid from Mexico

In Tokyo I saw workmen washing and drying city
buildings. Big buildings. Skyscrapers. They wore knee-high
booties with split toes and heavy canvas jodhpur like pants
while balancing on scaffolds, rags in hand. Very cool. I figure if we could get these uniforms we could lure a troop of
gym-boys to clean up New York City. Send them first to
the Empire State Building—for the publicity—and move
outward. Wash, wipe, revive.

Or better yet, we should involve everyone. New York-
ers are famous for complaining about how they don't have
yards. How about giving every New Yorker a single square
yard to care for and clean?

If your yard happened to fall on the side wall of a
building, imagine the adventure! Tromping through off-
limits offices or the boudoirs of the rich and famous,
swinging bucket and sponge. "Sorry for the interruption,

I've got to get to my yard." Customarily rude people would gratefully open their doors and happily serve you a cool beverage.

Those with street-level yards would scrub the gray-black sidewalks with brushes and bleach, revealing, I suspect, a completely new color scheme. Calcified dog-poop would chip away, pigeon droppings would no longer polka-dot the sidewalks. Those assigned underground territory could attack subway walls with pine-scented sprays. Impossible to imagine a fresh, sweet-smelling New York? I say do it now: A yard for every New Yorker.

But there's just one small problem: People rarely take care of something they don't own. In publicly owned areas, most everyone steps right over trash, broken glass, even people. Dirt, if it is not personal, not owned, simply slips through the cracks. (And stays there.) Besides, it would take about two seconds for your average New Yorker to find someone they could pay to clean up their single square yard.

I spent a month criss-crossing New York, with its vast but invisible custodial workforce. I am now convinced that the Statue of Liberty's torch should be replaced by a mop.

I mopped with the best, a veritable United Nations of cleaning: Violet, a student from Jamaica, Maria from Nicaragua, Antonia from Italy, and Susie from the Turks and Caicos. I cleaned with an Icelandic woman who assured me there was actually dust in her ice-capped country, though "less, *much* less" than here. I vacuumed with Brooklyn's

"Black Tornado," and chatted with Dean, who bills himself as the Gay Clean Machine, in an immaculate Chelsea kitchen where neither of us could find anything that vaguely warranted cleaning. "Some people have too much money," he drawled dramatically while spritzing the gleaming microwave with glass cleaner, "but as long as I get some of it, that's fine by me."

While cleaning up New York, I learned about world politics, the difficulty of finding work when you can't speak good English, and that it is crazy to take jobs with white floors. I discovered that most Manhattan refrigerators contain little to no food, typically only leftover takeout, most of which resembles modern art: colorful, intriguing, yet indefinable. New York refrigerators house vitamins, drugs, plastic pouches of condiments, and, I promise, men's underwear. Sometimes the whole story is in the medicine cabinet. Prozac is Manhattan popcorn.

I found that you can muck up an entire job by opening the windows on the way out. Rush-hour grime can mist all surfaces in a matter of moments. ("They ask me to leave the window open. What—are they *nuts*? 'Sure,' I tell them and then don't.")

New York cleaners earn between five and fifteen dollars an hour—off the books. Some get bonuses. Some charge for more hours than they've spent cleaning, but everyone must be careful of doormen who might tattle about skimping on time. (Bringing him a little something, a good cigar or a bottle of gin, I'm told, usually takes care of it.) Most cleaners don't do laundry. Some do. One cleaner was asked to save dryer lint; the client, an artist, was crafting a gorilla suit. Another cleaner was specifically asked to leave his coat on the floor in the hall, *not* in the closet. "What? Do they think I have fleas?" he asked, insulted by this request.

Some cleaners will never even meet their employers. Most people I met had been referred by a friend or a co-worker and were therefore entrusted with a key. Still, a key doesn't ensure security, for either the client or the cleaner. One day a neighbor reported a burglary, and a cleaner I know had to explain to the police, in his best accented English, why he was shifting around the furniture in a SoHo loft. He carefully avoided using the word *work* because, of course, he wasn't legal.

Even the dim-witted among us, those whose brain cells are stewed in ammonia, try to steer clear of jobs where people work at home.

On-the-clock cleaners who finish quickly watch cable or porn videos, nap, or make phone calls. The daring do laundry—their own. It's enjoyable to relax in a nice apartment three or four times the size of your own. And all, certainly most, do a good job. They have to. There are others eager for their jobs.

After all, in New York, what is enough money?

Pierre, who is black and gay and "Gives great bathroom—You can roll matzo balls in my tubs"—told me he is often tested. "A large wad of cash left on top of a dresser? Hel-*lo*. Like I'm gonna take it?"

One day I was helping Pierre with a fairly clean midtown apartment when we were surprised by the early return of his client, a New York editor clutching a feisty Chihuahua. While insisting that the pinstripes on her sheets be lined up, she learned I was a writer writing about cleaning. In her estimation this made me some sort of Dear Abby—type cleaning columnist.

"About this rattan sofa," she said, dragging me out of the bedroom, "Victor here has a penchant for peeing on it. It smells and it is stained. What should I do?"

Victor seemed quite agitated by my invading his territory. Over the sound of his growling and barking I made a suggestion: "Train the dog?"

Though Pierre earns more than his friends who work in galleries or sell clothes, he is embarrassed by his work.

"*All* of us should refuse to touch cat litter," he answered when I asked what he thought might make cleaning a more respectable form of employment.

"I'm so sick of going to a job and hearing that the last cleaner did the cat litter. I say to them, So where's that other cleaner *now*?" Pierre became quite serious. "I think we should organize. Organize, unionize, and say *no* to cat litter."

In fact, as I told Pierre, there had been an active household workers union in New York City. The Domestic Workers Union was first organized in Harlem in 1931 by a mixed group of Finnish and black women. It was set up to counteract the "slave marts," where unemployed women lined up on New York street corners each day hoping for work, for the day, for even an hour. The union had pushed for a $3.50-per-day minimum wage with a guaranteed lunch break, at a time when average pay ranged from ten to thirty cents per hour.

"Cat litter wasn't invented then," Pierre snipped, after listening intently to my history of the now long-gone union, "or it *would* have been a priority."

Many of the stories I heard in New York seemed similar, but one stood out enough to get me to the Upper West Side on a bitter, wet winter afternoon. Manhattan was nearly void of pedestrians; everyone was tucked into cabs or safely sequestered away from the wind and cold. Everyone, that is, except for a troop of black nannies, each pushing a high-tech stroller heaped with blankets and headed toward the park.

I was going to see Claudette, a Jamaican woman who cleans the Upper West Side apartment of one of my summer clients. Because Claudette's warm island country suffers from a poor economy, staying put meant a lifetime of scratching and scrimping. America promised riches, or at least a way to provide for her family. Leaving her three kids in Jamaica with her mother, Claudette landed in Brooklyn where she joined the leagues of foreigners who are swept out of their own countries only to end up sweeping up this one.

But my client had revealed to me the twist in Claudette's story: she had recently been awarded a twenty-something-million-dollar settlement in a lawsuit with one of New York's major hospitals. Eight years ago she'd given birth to a normal, healthy son, but the hospital had neglected the boy in some capacity, causing extensive brain damage. Because the hospital had appealed the amount (not the verdict), the money had yet to be awarded. In the meantime, Claudette was still cleaning.

My client, who swore by Claudette's work, was horrified that she might quit once the settlement came through. "She's really good," she said. "Like nobody else."

Would most cleaners quit if they suddenly came into several million dollars?

Before you could finger-snap in a wet pair of rubber gloves.

The bell on the apartment where Claudette was working was out of commission, so, as we had agreed, I called from the corner pay phone. When I rounded the corner Claudette popped her smiling face out the door, revealing a mouthful of gold and one diamond-studded tooth.

She was already at work upstairs so I followed her up the circular stairway. Though small, the apartment was exquisitely decorated, with lots of mirrors, glass, and gold velvet.

"I hate carpeted stairs," I said.

"Sure," Claudette agreed. "Carpeted stairs, *hard*."

It's great being able to make this kind of statement and not receive a questioning stare. Try saying "I hate carpeted stairs" to someone who programs computers, or sells stocks, or even teaches college English. You'll get a big, blank stare.

(Carpeted stairs means negotiating narrow steps while

awkwardly toting a heavy vacuum cleaner in one hand and pushing the wand with the other.)

After gleaning her first West Side client through an employment agency, Claudette's reputation spread and she was quickly connected. Though the clients paid the agency twenty dollars an hour, Claudette saw only five of that. She set out on her own when several clients offered to pay her directly. Now she had enough work, was paid well, and had few complaints.

Most cleaners get disturbed over something—one of my friends has a pet peeve about women's nightgowns; she literally gets nauseous if she has to pick one up, which she doesn't without an implement or rubber gloves. Claudette couldn't bear changing sheets.

"So I told them it's not so hard to do it themselves," she said. "Just pull off the dirty ones and spread out the clean ones." She had trained her clients well.

For the next few hours I watched Claudette clean. She was amazing. She actually picked up every item on the bathroom counter—each lipstick and can of deodorant —and wiped it off. (I myself just push everything aside, wipe, and replace; I don't even wipe my *own* lipsticks.) Claudette mopped the bathroom floor even though she had just done it two days ago and it looked perfectly clean.

With the clothes in the washer churning in the background, she told me she cleaned two houses a day at sixty-five dollars each.

"It's hard, sure," she said in her island sing-song. "But basically, I make a good living." *Basically* was said in four syllables, and traveled the range of an entire octave. On her wages, Claudette supports her family, including her five kids, who now live with her in Brooklyn. Plus, she makes enough to send money "home."

"People here don't think that way," she explained when I seemed shocked that she earned enough to share with her parents. "Only the rich man survives in Jamaica. It's hard down there, hard, sure. U.S. dollars can buy a lot in my country."

By the end of our time together Claudette had said *hard* maybe a hundred times. Life was hard. Work was hard. The weather was hard. The hardest thing about cleaning was ironing. She had a hard train commute. What happened to her baby boy was hard.

But one thing wasn't hard, and we both knew exactly how important that was: Claudette's clients were *easy*. All of them treated her well, both financially and personally. Unlike most housecleaners, she receives paid vacations, Christmas bonuses, and presents (sheets, towels, both castoffs and brand-new), most of which she sends to her parents. "Trust me, I'm lucky."

Claudette's sister is not so lucky. Her clients live on Long Island and she is paid what Claudette swears is the going rate out there: five dollars an hour. "Hard, sure," she agreed. "Forty, forty-five dollars a day? And *big* houses? A *long* train trip. I was *luck-y*."

I offered to clean but Claudette refused my help. She worked methodically around the apartment and I trailed.

In the bedroom, I peeked into a shopping bag and perused the books stacked by the bed.

"Do you spy?" I asked.

"Spy?"

"You know, look through their stuff. Read letters. Look at bills."

Claudette found this funny, though I could tell my sniffing around made her nervous. I opened the closet and suggested we try on some clothes. She laughed, not knowing me well enough to know I might be serious. I tried on several hats, and pointed out an ugly jumpsuit. "You should throw this out," I said. "Do the lady a favor."

We gossiped about our mutual client; both of us agreed she was aging well.

Finally, I asked the question I had come to ask. Would she really continue working when the money came through?

"I like my job."

"Come on, Claudette . . ."

"No, really, trust me, I enjoy my job. If I worked for anyone who didn't treat me right, I would leave that job. Trust me, I enjoy cleaning."

In a way, I do trust her. I myself like cleaning, though other people can't understand it, and it is often hard to explain why I like an activity other people find unbearable.

"I enjoy cleaning," she said again.

I nodded, she nodded, and for a moment our differences blurred.

"What will you do with the money?" I asked.

"Maybe buy a house on Long Island, or visit my parents," she said. "I've never been back to Jamaica."

It was almost dark when I left Claudette waiting by the dryer for the last round of towels to finish. The streets were still empty; residents wouldn't return home for hours. For most, a late dinner out meant they would do little more than sleep in these banks of cleaned apartments. People in this neighborhood probably worked in offices, where, as writers and agents and lawyers and financial planners and doctors (maybe some of them worked in the same hospital where Claudette's son had fallen through the cracks), they had little contact with people like Claudette. Did they realize their lipsticks had been dusted?

As I walked to the subway, braced against the cold, I wondered if there is a feeling of entitlement that accompanies having a regular housecleaner. I can only guess what it must be like to come home twice a week to a perfectly clean home. My train arrived, and as I took a seat I thought about whether people got used to having a clean home and stopped noticing that the housecleaner had come. I imagined what it would be like if one day we all switched roles. Cleaners got cleaned for and the cleaned for, cleaned. We have a secretary's day, a take-your-daughter-to-work day, how about a clean-for-your-cleaner day?

As we pulled away I saw Claudette reach the bottom of the subway steps, seconds too late for the Brooklyn-bound train. She didn't flinch or even frown. She simply took a seat on the platform and sunk into a bench. She looked hopeful and calm, despite the fact that she was headed home to a five-month-old baby, a mentally retarded eight-year-old, and several teenagers.

I wonder what Claudette, as a child, dreamed of doing with her life. I wonder if growing up on an island in this particular world economy means that one dreams simply of money, of getting out.

My childhood spy fantasy never seemed incongruous with my dreams of becoming president and owning a horse. I had yet to realize that women did not become presidents. I saved for the horse; worked a lemonade stand at the corner of our beachside street, selling two-cent cups of Kool-Aid and Oreos three for a nickel. At the end of an afternoon I'd have maybe sixty or eighty cents, double that if I was lucky enough to snare Mr. Atwell, a generous tipper, from inside his white Lincoln. I truly thought I would buy myself that horse. I stashed my money in a sock in my Barbie Dream House. This fist-sized cache attested to the possibility of my dream. Of course, I grew out of wanting a horse, but that sockful of change to this day is still packed away in my mother's garage, smashed in with Barbie's pink plastic Corvette and my Bicentennial red-white-and-blue high school graduation gown.

Over the course of my life, I have harbored a series of secret aspirations, some common to all kids, others more specific: to compete in the Olympics, to become a dentist, to marry David Bowie, to raise chickens, to invent something. My cycle of dreams and desires has often been exhausting, but these dreams are the luxury afforded to a certain number of Americans and, as a kid, I took advantage of them. I am now at that age where most things are not probable, nor even possible anymore.

Claudette assured me that she will keep cleaning, but I don't know about this. Once you throw out the obvious reasons for doing this kind of work—money, lack of education or opportunity—it's a riddle why any of us do what we do.

Cleaning Up My Life

*. . . by day I find release in grief and mourning
as I tend to household tasks, my women's work.*
—PENELOPE, *in* The Odyssey

I clean my own house often. I clean secretly. When I
am talking on the phone, sharing gossip, one hand is stir-
ring the toilet brush. I may be scouring the stovetop as my
friend tells me of her breakup. I may be fingering the dust
off baseboards at the moment another friend confesses her
affair. I am interested in their stories, but the moving of
dirt helps me process the information. In the midst of en-
tropy, of the decay of life and love, there is security in a
polished mirror. I may not see myself clearly, but I won't
see spattered toothpaste either.

My therapist is no stranger to dirt. Sometimes it's all I
can do not to get right up off the couch and empty the
wastebasket in her office. Hair on the carpet causes me to
wonder about the others who come to her with their tales
of woe.

One day, as I was lamenting over a traumatic relationship, I started to cry. (This relationship I refer to as my "ammonia and bleach" relationship: deadly, explosive, but with

astounding chemistry.) I reached for a tissue. I wiped. I moved to throw the tissue in the wastebasket. The basket was brimming. Suddenly, I couldn't bear putting my tissue on top of everyone else's. I picked up the basket and wandered around the office searching for a place to empty it while my therapist watched. The soiled tissues, piled one on the other, seemed like the evidence of modern life, the substance of suffering. I wanted only to dump the basket.

I stared at the tissues: some wadded, some crunched into tight balls. Others twisted longways like licorice sticks. Some like those origami cranes that people fold in hopes of peace. Someone, a woman I imagined, had shredded some into tiny bits.

I sat down with the basket on my lap. Bits of the torn tissue had floated out of the basket. They circled the room like bread crumbs on the blue carpet. A path leading where?

"Hansel and Gretel trying to get home," I said. "Can I empty this outside?"

She nodded.

Now, before my session begins, I empty the basket.

Cleaning helps me deal with the feelings in my body.

Sometimes cleaning is a task to do. Like writing a letter. One day I woke up, and in that early-morning half-awake state, I felt something was off, as if my house were dirty or my laundry piled in huge mounds. But all chores were completed. Then it came to me—Bill's name and Ken's face—and I knew that to get my life cleaned up I had to write a difficult letter.

Ken was a friend of mine in college, a dear friend whom I had kept loose contact with over the years. Bill was his longtime lover. Several months ago, I had called Ken's office at the Palm Springs hospital where he worked as di rector of psychological services. It was a simple idea: to call with my annual holiday greeting. I was transferred so many times to hesitating secretaries and administrators that I knew something was terribly amiss. By the time the last person got on the phone and asked me about the nature of my relationship with Ken—personal or professional?—I was already without breath.

Ken had died.

> Dear Bill,
>
> I am sorry it has taken me so long to get in touch with you.
>
> My delinquency about contacting you has everything to do with my refusal to believe that Ken is actually dead. By not making contact, I could hold on to my picture-postcard version of your still intact and, to me, terribly romantic Palm Springs life: Ken speeding around the flat, glaring city in that over-the-top yellow Cadillac; Ken retrieving

blown-down palm fronds from the saccharine blue pool; Ken serving drinks in the afternoon shade on the sun porch.

It's an understatement to say I was shocked by news of Ken's death. Ken was someone whom I rarely saw, yet I completely counted on him being there. I imagined that we would continue to meet up every few years and run through our litany of foibles: I would complain about my most recent break-up, he would moan and whine about your working too much. Maybe when we were older, we could go on one of those silly cruises and both you and he would slay me with your wry, cruel observations of our fellow shipmates and play shuffleboard. Here at my computer, I ground myself in details—desk, chair, Ken not being here—so I will stop pretending we might someday be drinking ridiculous fruit cocktails aboard some ship, in some other future.

Ken was a witness to my coming of age. He observed (sometimes uncritically, usually with biting sarcasm) my struggle to forge some sort of identity. You know the story we made up together: our private joke about the perfect American family, "The Mondellos." There we were, Ken and I, two naive, overprotected suburban kids, eighteen? nineteen? years old, in France of all places, looking like refugees from an L. L. Bean catalog, which is to say, we didn't blend in with the *je ne sais quois* style of the Southern French countryside. Our outfits were bad, our accents worse. Neither of us (me more than him) knew what we were doing there. Both of us wanted to have a foreign affair, with the same guy, I think. What we got instead was a pervert outside our dorm rooms flashing his privates at us. This scared me, but it amused Ken quite a bit and he pointed and embarrassed the guy into leaving.

The Mondellos were our make-believe family, from Muncie, Indiana. Harold (Ken), Doris (me), and our preteen daughter, Dottie (Barbara S.). The story we made up was that the Mondellos had shipped their Country Squire station wagon to "The Old Country" for their *gran tour d'Europe*. The Mondellos were only as obnoxious as the tourists we actually observed. ("You mean you don't take American dollars? These Eye-talians don't take greenbacks!") We used "hubby" and "the little woman" as endearments, and addressed each other as Harold and Doris for years after our trip. I re-

ceived a Christmas card from Ken several years
ago signed "your ex-husband, Harold." And when
Ken came out to me we laughed about my husband having to "find himself" and my going on
Donahue as "Wife whose husband left her for a
MAN!" "You're no longer the little woman, Doris,"
he hissed. "I am."

I loved it when you both came to visit several
years ago and we went to that men's leather bar
where there were giant dildoes hanging over the
bar. I couldn't tell what they were and Ken said, go
see what those things are, as if he didn't already
know. I came nose-to-nose with a twenty-incher as
fat as my arm. I drew back grimacing. "Doris, pick
a prick!" he barked. The bartender, although I
knew him, and actually had cleaned his house
once, looked askance at me as I slunk to the back
of the dark, sticky room. There were no other
women there and men without shirts murmured in
the corners. There was a back room, though even
I, *voyeur extraordinaire*, was too shy to venture in.
"Harold, do you really think I should be in here?"
"No," he replied, with that slightly evil laugh of
his. He had already made friends with everybody
there, received free drinks from the coolly distant

bartender, and he knew they could laugh about me later, when he returned and sat at the bar telling stories.

That bartender and his partner are dead now.

I can't bear it, living in these times, though as we know, everybody feels the same way and now it's trite to be dramatic about these commonplace things, death and loss. Still, Ken is the first one who will be specifically missed by me; the rest are names and faces and stories that don't actually intersect with the crucial bar graph of my life.

Though Ken and I had little contact over the past few years, even from afar I felt comforted by him being a therapist. It was as though I had my own private shrink out there, on call. One time, when the going got really rough, I called him for advice. He had no idea where I was in my life at that point, but he listened and from across the country I felt better.

What I am trying to say is that Ken meant more to me than I ever let him know. Your home out there in that wide desert, with your own twenty-three—or was it twenty-six?—palm trees, seemed to me like it should have been safe from disease and death. After all, Palm Springs is where

old people live. Palm Springs is where septuage-
narians with tanned and wrinkled faces scoot about
on golf carts, early-bird dinners are de rigeur,
where sixty-year-olds are bagging groceries. Not a
place for a not yet forty-year-old man with a buff
body to die during a Californian winter.

I feel better now, as if I had cleaned my house,
though writing this was a good deal more difficult
than vacuuming or dusting.

AIDS compels me to clean. In this I am not alone.
One dying man I know spent thousands of dollars for an
exterminator so that he could die in a bug-free home. It
was his last effort on earth; after the exterminator left, he
slid into dementia. Another infected friend vacuums three
or four times a day, wringing his hands when the floor is
dirty like some sort of cross-dressed Lady Macbeth.

A mother with a son who has AIDS has scrubbed the
finish off her stove. Her son calling to chat was told, "I
can't talk now, I'm disinfecting the suitcases."

The prescription for a clean slate: scour away fear.

I have cleaned for five people who are now dead. I
don't know why this high ratio—is it due to chance? loca-
tion?—but it's not something I tell new clients.

Week to week I have seen the signs of letting go. I vacuum around respirators, dust battalions of pill bottles.

One day I sat on the bed with a dying woman. Full of
chemicals, she was bald and wouldn't let me see her head.

She wore a huge, floppy, battered straw hat. Her round, hairless face reminded me of a Cabbage Patch doll. I had just been dumped by my girlfriend.

"Honey," she told me, "life is short. Find some love."

We both cried, the vacuum whirring in place, the smell of sickness and Endust mingling to evoke in me a slight nausea. I wanted to hug her, but didn't. She died the next week.

Another client was an agent summering in a million-dollar beach house with his standard poodle, who often joined him in his lukewarm hot tub. I took names from his Rolodex. I called Joni Mitchell at her Malibu home and Nastassja Kinski in Rome. I left messages. I asked Joni to call my best friend and sing her happy birthday. She never called.

He didn't know I knew he was dying. But I know prescriptions. I know insurance forms. Still, it's nice to have a clean house to come home to, or to leave from.

A Yen for Cleaning

Who is the foe for whom they attack
With rag a brush and pail?
'Tis dust—but not seen dirt alone:
The heart's dust they assail.
—ROKUMANGYOGAN, *"The Army of Peace"*

Some people vacation in Yellowstone, Aruba, or New Orleans. Others go to Bali to lie on white beaches, or to the Himalayas to climb steep mountains. I went to Japan to clean toilets.

I heard about a group of cleaning people in Japan through a friend, who connected me with Sho Ishikawa. Sho, about forty, now lives in Manhattan but had been raised in Japan as a member of a cleaning commune. His parents, who had spent most of their lives in the commune, still live there, and his father is one of the present spiritual leaders.

"It is difficult to imagine cleaning for your whole life," Sho said in the first of several phone conversations. "Growing up, I felt like there was a dark cloud over my head." Sho always knew he would leave the commune, and as soon as he finished school he took off for New York to

become a Buddhist monk. After a number of years he left
the Zen community, and he's now working in the world of
public accounting. Sho became the gatekeeper to my exotic
experience. He tried to explain the history of the group.

Ittoen ("One Light" or "One Lamp Garden") is rooted
in the spiritual awakening, teachings, and life example of
Tenko Nishida (1872–1968). Followers worship Nishida's Oneness of Light philosophy while embracing all spir-
itualities based in the desire for peace and grounded in the
ideal of humble service. (Both Buddha and Christ lived the
life of the homeless, I was reminded later, and both washed
the feet of others.)

Sho sketched out the life of Tenko-san, as he is referred to by most. In the late 1800s, Tenko-san, a failing
land developer, became dissatisfied by the corruption of
capitalism. Unwilling to struggle against others for his
own survival, he challenged the accepted assumption that
one worked in order to live. Tenko-san's awakening occurred after three days of meditation and an insight about
the deep, natural bonding between mothers and children.
This relationship became the metaphor he used to explain
the pure interdependence people could have, both with
each other and with "the light," or God. Life was given
freely to all and was not something that had to be worked
for; work was therefore a way of offering thanksgiving for
the gift of life.

Renouncing his family, status, and all possessions,
Tenko-san began to serve others. He lived a simple life,
scrubbing, mopping, chopping wood, and cleaning what

were then rudimentary privies. In return, he was offered food and shelter, even money. Declining all but the bare necessities, giving service became the way he connected with others. For him, this was enlightenment.

Over the next ten years, Tenko-san attracted followers, and together they lived what he called the life of the "homeless." In 1928, some land outside of Kyoto was donated for the establishment of a community. In the fifties and sixties, the commune had hundreds of members; now, nearly thirty years after Tenko-san's death, only about 150 disciples remain.

I don't think Sho quite knew why I wanted to travel ten thousand miles to scrub toilets with a bunch of people I couldn't even communicate with, and I wasn't quite sure myself. Nevertheless, after a succession of phone calls to Japan, a weeklong visit was arranged that would culminate on the national Day of Labor, a day the entire community went cleaning. Sho's own English teacher, a woman close to seventy who had lived over forty years in the commune, would be my official host.

In preparation for this adventure, I attempted to learn a handful of the many Japanese words for *dirty*. In addition to the basic word for *dirty*, *kitanai*, the Japanese language offered a plethora of delightfully onomatopoeic names, each detailing the various kinds and ways things could be soiled. *Gicho-gicho*, dripping with grease, sounded much more disgusting than *gucho-gucho*, messed up or jumbled. My favorite, which I chanted one day while wiping sludge from behind a toilet, was *nuru-nuru,* "slimy." Hopeless at languages, out of my unwieldly mouth the word *shimikomu,* the specific term for ground-in grime, sounded like a whale at an amusement park.

Japan itself was astoundingly clean. Before my week with the cleaners, I spent some time in Tokyo, during which I became thoroughly convinced that I lived in the wrong country. Litter? No. Graffiti? No. Clean people. Clean cars, buses, and streets. Trains were not only spotless, on time, and pleasant smelling, they were carpeted and *upholstered.* (Imagine, if you can, a New York subway carpet after a day of commuters.) People with colds considerately donned face masks, and poop-scooping for pet dogs was fastidiously executed with tiny shovels and rakes.

But all this cleanliness seemed occasionally to lead to excess. The first time I entered a department store bathroom I was shocked to hear the sound of a flushing toilet as I sat down, *before* I went. I jumped, alarmed at the possibility of being doused from underneath, but there was no whirlpool below, only calm waters. I sat down again, warily, and the phantom flushing resumed.

The next toilet I sat upon sang like a babbling brook. The next, at the contemporary museum, simulated the flow of running tap water. Finally, with difficulty and slightly obscene charades, I learned that many Japanese women were embarrassed by the sound of peeing, and had become accustomed to flushing on the way into the toilet in order to shroud evidence of their bodily functions. This doubled water usage, and officials, fearing shortages, joined engineers in developing the camouflaging toilets. Extreme, yes, but I would graciously accept the trade-off. Sweet-smelling taxis with soft, plush seats, lace doilies on the headrests, and complimentary Kleenex?

I could live with babbling toilets.

By the time I had made my way to the cleaning compound, I had begun to recognize Japan's contradictory nature. Sure, everything was squeaky-clean, yet you can buy dirty underpants, supposedly soiled by genuine schoolgirls, from streetside vending machines. And, though nobody seemed able or willing to speak English, English was absolutely everywhere, albeit oddly configured. "Let's Wedding" announced a bridal shop advertisement, while my brand of coffee was called Blendy. The powdered creamer? Creap. A popular beverage slung the off-putting slogan "Sweat drink!" and the cigarette billboards proclaimed "Today I Smoke." I bought a thermos so I could brew up my own Blendy and Creap (the four-dollar coffee was busting me). The thermos was named Twinkleheart and the tag promised "Fall in love with twinkleheart and she becomes charming happiness for awhile."

I hoped so. I was starting to feel lonely.

The day I was due at Ittoen, I was riddled with apprehension. I still knew little of where I was going or what I'd be doing. At a Kyoto marketplace, a fishmonger asked me where I was staying. I told him and he made gestures as if he were sweeping with a broom. I nodded. He bowed, low, then gathered up sellers from the neighboring stalls. A volley of Japanese nods ensued. Soon I was surrounded by a half-circle of bobbing bowers. One woman gave me a strange green Japanese pastry, and another forced upon me what seemed like a package of dried fish fins. Bowing while shuffling backward, I tripped and nearly landed in a box of spiky sea urchins. The hoopla made me a little nervous. I wondered what kind of cult I was staying with.

I pondered how to spend the few short hours I had left before I needed to board the commuter train that would take me from Kyoto to Ittoen. Meditation at one of Kyoto's famous temples? Quiet contemplation over a cup of green tea?

Hardly. I had read all my books, and suddenly, the thought of a week without reading matter made me panic. Map in hand, I struggled to find a bookstore that sold used English titles. The one shop I found had slim pickings, which forced me to buy several volumes I'd be embarrassed to carry stateside. The most promising one was *Best American Sports Stories*, several years out of date.

I still had two full packs of sugar-free bubble gum I'd brought from home. Provisions intact, I was ready. At the last minute I bought a bag of M&M's at the train station's Let's Kiosk; chocolate might console me if things went badly.

Ittoen was tucked into the hills east of Kyoto; gorgeously kept grounds hugged a mishmash of buildings. A brand-new high-tech semi-high-rise sidled up next to a

cluster of traditional Japanese bungalows with thatched
roofs and curling corners. I entered the compound feeling
renewed confidence. I was quite relieved to find that the
place actually existed.

Outside the office, which resembled a typical bank
office—faxes, copiers, computers, and phones—I met
Sho's teacher, Ayako Isayama, a slight, short-haired woman,
in a black karate like *gi*. She politely invited me to follow
her to my room, taking off at such a clip that in order to
keep up I was forced into a gallop. If I hadn't known her
age, I'd have guessed about half. Who said that cleaning
aged a person quickly? Even her hands were youthful.

The grounds we passed through were impeccably
groomed; maples and mossy rolling hills, a small brook
snaking through the center of the many buildings. Several
older women, similarly dressed, swept leaves with traditional bamboo brooms and exchanged words with Ayako
as we made our way up a forest path. I was introduced as
Sho's friend, though I hadn't even met him yet. Nevertheless, I nodded and said, "Good!" each time I was asked,
"Sho, good?"

I was taken aback by the largeness of the whole place.
From Sho's description, I had imagined a small group of
dedicated toilet cleaners living in spartan quarters, buckets
and sponges always at hand. Instead, I found a highly organized group that ran what was essentially a small town
with its own complicated economy. I would soon learn
that the commune supported itself by operating various
businesses, including a school for every age group (avail-

able to those on "the outside" as well to members), a printing press, an agricultural program, a theater and performance group, as well as a "theme park" located in a southern province. The park, dedicated to the theme of peace, featured replicas of Easter Island statuettes and a huge "Peace Bell," which, according to Ayako, resonated with a beautifully calming tone.

The group also facilitated training sessions for young factory workers and business people, and as we approached the building in which I was to stay, we encountered a single-file line of *gi*-clad men and women who looked, as they jogged past, to be in their early twenties. Though it was late afternoon and the fall air was crisp and chilling, they wore their flip-flops barefooted, without *tabi*, the split-toed Japanese socks.

"Mr. Donut workers," Ayako explained, "returned from *gyogan*, humble toilet cleaning."

I loved Mr. Donut. Not only was it the only place in Japan that offered free refills on coffee, but the employees would greet each customer with a bow and a phrase something like: "I am your servant. How may I humbly serve you?" Even in the overly polite, ever-gracious world of Japanese commerce (where I had the best Big Mac I've ever had served to me *at my table* by the nicest, cleanest, most pleasant McDonald's worker I have ever met), an average Mr. Donut employee stood head-and-shoulders above the others. I had once passed a Mr. Donut shop just before it opened and saw the whole group of workers, heads bowed, chanting what seemed to be a prayer of thankfulness.

"Four days' training. Humble toilet cleaning, door-to-door service," Ayako explained.

More inquiry revealed that four thousand Mr. Donut workers spent time at Ittoen each year; the training was aimed to promote humility and facilitate group dynamics. For toilet cleaning they were assigned specific houses in nearby towns. And they would seek out a variety of other tasks—washing clothes, babysitting, weeding—wherever they were needed, undertaking such service in the tradition of *takuhatsu*, "road-side service," like the "begging-bowl rounds" practiced by Zen monks, who still visit households to recite religious chants. In the afternoons they worked at Ittoen, gathering wood, clearing fields, and tending the gardens. The last day was spent reflecting on their training.

I marveled as the group passed. It's a stretch for me to imagine a group of American workers, say from Dunkin' Donuts or Burger King, jogging door-to-door, heads bowed, begging to clean toilets.

The building in which I was to stay was old, one of the original ones donated in the thirties by a "Friend of Light," one of the many people who lived elsewhere in Japan and supported the group financially and materially. I settled into my room, a sparse square covered in *tatami* mats and centered with a *kotatsu*—a table with a heater attached underneath. The *kotatsu* was the only furniture in the room, as well as the sole source of heat. By now, late afternoon, the room was already frigid. Ayako switched on the table and demonstrated how to sit tucked under its overhanging blankets. Over the next week I spent many hours squeezing as much of myself as far under the table as possible, bending and twisting like a yogi so that more of me might glean a little warmth.

That night Ayako made dinner in the quiet, dark kitchen in our huge and, except for us, empty dormitory. We chatted in simple English. Ayako's skills were more than adequate; however, our cultural differences made the conversation stilted. I asked if I might be able to clean with the Mr. Donut trainees.

Ayako, considering my request, looked away from me. "Difficult, with no Japanese," she shorthanded. "May not be possible."

She rose and began to wash the dishes. I noticed how dirty the kitchen was, the walls spotted with oil and grease, not at all how I had imagined it would be.

"Saturday," she said. "You clean Saturday, with the group."

It was Monday.

"Morning service at five-thirty," she announced and disappeared behind the sliding door to her room. That first night I set the *kotatsu* over my futon, although it was surely a fire risk. At least my toes wouldn't freeze.

If somewhere there is a record for speed-changing shoes, Ayako must hold it. As at every Japanese house, each time we entered our building, we left our street shoes at the front door and put on what were essentially bedroom slippers. Slippers came off before entering *tatami* rooms, where socks were the appropriate footwear. Hundreds of these changes happened every day, and Ayako made each as smoothly as if she were an Olympian passing a baton. I stumbled and fumbled, often catching myself with a socked toe on the foyer—a definite no-no. (But because my feet were so often aired, I was pleased to have packed many pairs of clean, fresh-smelling socks.)

At dawn's light I followed Ayako down the dusky corridor of our ancient building, where after my first shoe mishap of the day (still sleepy, I nearly toppled over while making the change), she sped off toward the Spirit Hall. I loped to catch up.

Inside the bare wood hall, both Buddhist and Christian images flanked the altar. At center position was a round window overlooking a view of the forest. Ittoen elders and Mr. Donut people lined up on both sides of the room, settled in *seiza* (kneeling, heels under buttocks) on *tatami* platforms, men on one side and women on the other. I took a seat behind Ayako. Everyone looked more comfortable than me. My ankles and joints started to ache after only a few minutes. With some relief, I noticed, several of the Mr. Donut youngsters began to fidget after a while, though the women in front of me, a few who had to have been over eighty, looked like they could sit folded up origami-wise for hours.

Orchestrated by the current leader—Tenko-san's grandson, a tall, pleasant-looking man of about fifty—the service was both calming and invigorating. We began with a song recounting Ittoen history, and then chanted a semiobscure Buddhist *sutra*, the gist of which is nonattachment to worldly goods. Morning stretches were performed to the accompaniment of a resounding "*ooomm,*" which grew even louder with each repetition.

After the service I raced behind Ayako back to our place, where she offered me a choice of toilet brush or broom. I chose the brush and was handed a bucket and rag. Both the squat toilet and the two standard toilets were fairly clean, but I did the job well, as I had the notion that I would be judged as a person on the quality of my cleaning. By the end of the week I realized this was stupid, but that first day I practically took the finish off the porcelain and wiped every inch of the wooden stalls and floors.

Ayako set off to mop the entire building and was, of course, finished before me. Experience and a lifetime of cleaning, I told myself consolingly.

Breakfast—miso soup, rice, warmed bits of various vegetables, dried indistinguishable fruit, and green tea— seemed at first frighteningly unrelated to my usual fare (coffee and toast), but the warm food in the unheated building actually tasted good. Emulating Ayako, who cites the hundreds starving in Rwanda as one reason she never wastes even a morsel of food, I ate everything on my plate. I marveled at the tastiness of the rice, finding the speckled gruel unusually savory. Upon inspection, however, I discovered tiny fish heads, half the size of a grain of rice. I swallowed deliberately, eyes and all. That week I put many things in my mouth I wished I hadn't. Only by the third day did I find myself seriously daydreaming about pizza.

After breakfast I was free till morning teatime.

"What should I clean?" I asked, as I finished drying the breakfast dishes.

Ayako seemed puzzled by my request and gave me a book about Ittoen, in English, before retreating into her room to tackle stacks of correspondence and translations.

I set upon the kitchen, tackling the counters and scouring the walls with a wire brush and Look!, a Japanese cleanser (which for some reason is pronounced *Rooku*), until I thought they might crumble. Apparently some foreign boarders had recently lived in the building, Ayako reported, and they cooked with gallons of oil and were not into cleaning. Four hours later I had only finished half the area.

"Very nice, much better now," Ayako said, pouring us glasses of thin, sweet yogurt. "Funny American who likes to clean!"

Ayako was the only English speaker in the group, and my Japanese still consisted of that silly dirt vocabulary and a fluent "thank you" and "thank you very much." We ate together, and when we weren't eating in the central dining room (where food was eaten on hardwood floors in *seiza*, in silence, and downed in minutes), she told me stories of her life. Although I thought I had a good understanding of cleaning, it became clear I was completely out of my league.

Ittoen as a community had clearly passed its prime and the dwindling population seemed to portend its eventual demise, but the philosophy—nonattachment and service to others—seemed timeless, if not ideal. Members own little personal property, and although each receives a monthly allowance, all other assets are held in trust. Upon joining, all possessions are left behind.

Ayako didn't have much to give up when she joined, at least materially. Born in 1927 into a prosperous family, her parents had lost their land in post–World War II redistribution. A student at a Christian college, Ayako was "terribly depressed and searching." When she discovered Tenko-san's book *The Life of Penitence*, which described his journey from miserable wealthy businessman to humble servant, she immediately knew she had to live that kind of life.

"Either that or die," she explained. "I was weak and did not have the will to live. The world made me very sad."

Unfortunately, Ayako's parents refused to let her join the group, which at that point had already situated itself on the hillside where it now stands. So Ayako spent the next few years teaching English in nearby Kyoto, living by Ittoen principles—serving without remuneration—often sleeping in her schoolroom and visiting the group when possible. Eventually she joined the community and was immediately disowned by her family. Ayako soon became Tenko-san's official secretary, right-hand disciple, and host to foreign guests, working tirelessly at home and traveling overseas twenty times over the last forty years to share Ittoen's ideals at international religion and peace conferences.

One evening, after a light meal of fish soup, dried figs, and rice, I flipped through the pages of one of Ayako's many scrapbooks while she talked about her life. She spoke of her own spiritual awakening, which literally happened after cleaning a toilet.

"There were lots of spider webs on the ceiling and walls. Mud was piled on the floor. The stool was dirty. I swept the cobwebs and began to scrub. After about thirty minutes the grain of the floor came to be seen and the stool became white. I felt refreshed. Wiping my sweat, I looked behind me and saw the lady of the house chanting Buddha's name, her hands in prayer. It was a meeting of two persons, in prayer and in peace. I went outside and saw a tiny blue flower blooming by the roadside. It was so beautiful! I talked with the blue flower, just like I am talking to you."

I nodded, but never in my toilet-cleaning life had I ever come close to this kind of feeling, or spoken to a flower.

"In my heart I saw a big tree, with everything in its branches. You, me, air, birds, flowers. I knew everything was related. That was my realization after cleaning that toilet."

I flipped pages, the photos dated back decades. Many pictures documented *roto*, the "life of the homeless," and showed lines of uniformed disciples marching across the countryside or through small Japanese villages. In these, Ayako was often at the head of the group, beside Tenko-san, a man who even in pictures had a powerful, transcendent look. Thin, serious, yet with an open countenance, Tenko-san was usually photographed with a bucket and toilet rag.

"Were you ever scared?" I asked. "Not knowing where'd you end up each night?"

"Once," she said. "In America." She pulled an album from the bottom of the stack. Inside, there were pictures of Ayako with American families, some on a farm and one next to a Washington, D.C., apartment building. And there were newspaper clippings, from the mid-seventies, about a young Japanese "nun" who had volunteered to massage feet at several retirement homes.

"For over one month I did humble service. I spent six dollars," she said. "Two dollars I gave to a church," she added.

I drew out the whole story, beginning with Ayako's middle-of-the-night arrival at New York's JFK airport and the kind black taxi driver who carted her free to Manhattan at the end of his shift. At Penn Station, while waiting for a bus to rural New Jersey, she cleaned toilets and massaged the feet of a homeless woman. It was in New Jersey, during a four-hour trek down a country road, when Ayako had felt afraid. She didn't know where she was going and felt so lonely she almost cried. She passed fields dotted with cows, and most of the farmhouses she saw were uninhabited. When she finally stumbled onto a family home, she explained her mission to the woman of the house simply. "I live in Japan. My work is to help people. May I work for you?" she asked, with her hands in a gesture of prayer.

After a discussion with her husband, this woman welcomed Ayako into their home. Ayako then accompanied her to the grocery store, riding in a car back down the road she had just walked. "I was passing the same cows, thinking I had just been so sad and alone," she told me. "Now I was happy and completely taken care of!"

Ayako stayed at this house almost a week, cleaning, cooking Japanese food, and working in the garden. "They asked me always to pray over their food," she said, translating the Ittoen grace: "True faithfulness consists of doing service for others and ignoring your own interests." This couple arranged for her to spend time with friends, and these folks sent her to others. At each home, she cooked, cleaned, babysat, and by example, spread Tenko-san's philosophy.

One night, while staying in a neighborhood in D.C., she strayed into an iffy part of town. A local beat cop warned her to be careful, but Ayako kept walking.

"I met three black girls who said, 'Chinese lady, you are small but you are charming!' This made me laugh so I wasn't afraid."

Later that evening, when approached by a group of young men, she admits to having felt a little nervous. "I didn't want to meet them, but then one turned around and said 'Nice jacket,'" Ayako paused. "I was very happy then."

Ayako's pureness of spirit was alternately inspiring and defeating. I could not *imagine* going door-to-door in America asking for the "humble service of cleaning toilets." Yet buoyed by her example, I asked several more times about going door-to-door here in Japan. Each time she seemed evasive. Aside from our morning duties, and some translating and writing she requested help with, my time was my own. I felt frustrated; I feared I was going to miss out on the pure Ittoen experience.

But did I need someone to *assign* me to clean? Couldn't I take the initiative myself, even go into town on my own? I had the outfit, my *gi*-top and my headscarf with its large calligraphed circle of "nothingness." But the thought of knocking on a Japanese door without a translator was daunting. Would they invite me into their toilets? It was doubtful. Still, if I had a pure enough heart?

But did I?

I set about local tasks instead. I tutored English to some teens at the high school and sat in on primary school classes where the newly arrived American teacher tried to teach vocabulary about emotions. Her analogies whizzed completely over the students' heads. "Jealous!" she attempted enthusiastically, with her eyes squinched up. "Like if someone buys the new sweater *you* wanted." Stone faces. In a moneyless community based on nonattachment and peace, I thought she might consider rethinking her lesson.

I de-greased most of the kitchen, and each day spent some time outside sweeping up leaves with a bamboo broom. I felt a little jealous watching the Mr. Donut people jog past, buckets bouncing. I had yet to penetrate the elusive Japanese home.

Occasionally, however, meditating on the task at hand, I did experience something like a moment of cleaning bliss. This feeling was larger and fuller than the at-home experiences of pleasure I've had cleaning for others. Besides, I noted, my at-home work was usually followed by a big fat check and accolades from my clients.

One afternoon I set about clearing the paths of downed maple leaves and fishing mounds of drowned yellow-and-gold fallen foliage from the fish pond. Watching the carp scatter, I dipped my broom and pulled debris from the pond's rippling surface. The sun worked its way through four layers of woollies, and for the first time that week I warmed up.

I piled leaves all afternoon, transferring them to the wheelbarrow and carting them to the bathhouse where they'd be burned to heat the steamy water for my evening scrub. Each time I returned up the path, several women, also with brooms, waved and bowed. Five or six hours passed gently and without effort. Everything felt right with the world. I thought I might return to Ittoen for a year, or perhaps two! Cleaning and eating well, working without being worried about money, fame, or getting ahead. What else would I do with my life? The well-swept garden looked like a mossy felt carpet rising and falling, while reflections of the billowy clouds floated across the pond.

Then the wind came up.

Within seconds the ground was covered, and I mean *covered*, with leaves. A mass of orange maple leaves shrouded the pond. Carp? Where? The reversal of my efforts took about thirteen seconds. As the noisy wind decimated all evidence of my work, the sun sunk behind the mountain. Suddenly chilled, I shuddered.

The women down the lane simply withdrew into their houses, bowing to each other on retreat. As the rain of leaves continued, I started to cry.

I wondered: If a forest is swept and no one sees it, was it ever really swept?

I wondered: Would I ever stop trying to achieve Home Ec Student of the Year?

Later, after I pulled myself together in the privacy of my room, I escaped to the nearby town, scuttling down the mountain path in the growing darkness. At the bakery, I bought a chocolate éclair.

At 6:30 A.M. on Saturday about seventy people gathered on the school grounds, each dressed in full Ittoen gear and carrying buckets and brooms. Our destination was in Osaka where, as a group, we'd clean a large Buddhist temple. Ayako, who had been on a similar field trip a week earlier, had been asked to stay home and sweep the garden. I was delivered to Sho's mother, a beautiful gray-haired woman I suspected to be about sixty. She spoke little English. We smiled and nodded while teams were arranged, and buckets and brooms rearranged. My team was made up of seven elderly men and women.

Next to us, a group of teenagers kidded around with each other innocently. One girl I had tutored laughed at the sight of me in my *gi* and official Ittoen head wrap. "*You* clean toilets?" she asked, and her shyer friends giggled behind her.

After Tenko-san's official toilet cleaning poem was

recited, we marched out of the compound in a single line, while elders and those staying behind bowed us on our way. With Ittoen flags flying and buckets looped over left arms, we filed down to the nearby town where our buses waited. I followed Sho's mother, actually quite delighted to be a soldier in an army of cleaners!

Arriving in Osaka around eight, we were welcomed by a group of Buddhist priests and a group of lay supporters ready to join us for the day's work. After a brief service and a lot of bowing, each group was given a map and set to task. The teenaged groups headed off to the banks of public toilets, and I gazed longingly in their direction. My team was escorted to a graveled area about the size of a football field and I was given a bamboo broom. I looked around. At first look the ground seemed clean, but closer inspection revealed tiny leaves, cigarette butts, and scraps of litter. My team attacked immediately, each sweeping with abandon and, I soon discovered, great skill.

And it immediately became clear that I lacked this skill. Sweep too hard and the gravel comes up, producing a mound of gravel, leaves, dirt, and trash while leaving bald patches of bare ground. Sweep lightly and nothing moves: both gravel and leaves stay put. I watched as members of my team flicked their brooms expertly with the precise amount of *oomph*. It was as if the bristles of their brooms were programmed to know exactly which particles should be gathered and which left behind. In hopes of getting the "trick," I experimented with left-handed, right-handed, and back-handed techniques. I tried side-to-side and up-and-back. After an hour, I had barely swept a quarter of the area the others had done. The sun came out strong; I was sweating. My head itched.

Temple viewing ranks highly as a national holiday pastime, and soon well-dressed Japanese visitors began to arrive at the temple grounds. I watched for signs: Were we regarded with disgust or skepticism, like a band of chanting Hare Krishnas or over-solicitous Moonies? Some people stopped to watch, and as a foreigner, I was particularly scrutinized. Several people bowed; one woman asked if this was "my job." I told her no, "volunteer." She cocked her head, quizzically. Mostly we were ignored.

Our team covered the grounds like a pack of grazing sheep, and the gravel really did look a whole lot better after we had swept through. As we approached a particularly dirty and trash-laden area, I noticed a group of men sprawled on some stairs outside an abandoned building. After discovering bottles and food in the weeds edging the walkway, I realized these men were homeless. Even at this early hour, most had been drinking. Red-faced and weary, they watched us work. It made me nervous.

As we neared, several men got up and began tidying up the area, throwing trash in the bins and stacking empty bottles. I was amazed. I remembered something Ayako had told me about Tenko-san. In his day, when down-and-outs came to Ittoen, as many did following the war's devastation, each was welcomed and given food and shelter. But after two days, they were required to join work groups or do *roto*. Tenko-san believed handouts would brew resentment and keep people disempowered. Work would reveal a heart of thanksgiving. Here, it seemed obvious that our example had prompted these men to action. One man nodded as I passed.

We continued past the steps until we had covered the whole area. Our leader, a man as slim and firm as a beetle and probably eighty years old, led us tirelessly to an area near a turtle pond. We swept some more. My hands hurt; I suspected blisters were forming on my palms. At times I felt bone-tired, and then a new energy would surprisingly appear. After four hours, I saw other Ittoen groups heading back to the main temple, but our geriatric team seemed intent on working until the last possible moment.

Over the morning I felt like my sweeping was improving, but at quitting time, while working near a small grove of trees that had obviously been used as a toilet, I realized that either Sho's mother or her robust friend had always been working some distance behind me. I looked at the path I'd cleared, and then at the ground they had passed over. Shards of leaves and a tiny confetti of trash spotted my work. Where they had swept, the ground was pristine: a carpet of smooth, gray rock.

They'd swept over every place I'd covered.

Suddenly, I was *really* tired.

We carted our brooms and bags to the main temple, and after a short service with the Buddhists (during which the teens nodded off, miraculously, still seated in *seiza*), we were fed fish-head rice rolls. Before boarding the bus, I stopped to use the bathroom. Twenty or thirty stalls lined up, each with a squat toilet inside. Though they obviously had been recently cleaned, and water still shone on the slick tiled walls, many people, both homeless and visitors to the temple, had already been through. After only several hours of use, they were already dirty. As I exited my stall, a man threw up all over the floor.

On the bus ride back to Ittoen, the skyscrapers of Osaka disappearing behind me, I questioned if I was capable of selfless cleaning. There was certainly no reason I couldn't clean public places, say toilets in the park or even the sidewalks on my street. On my next trip to New York, I could carry a bottle of spray and wipe down subway seats; I could do an entire car in the time it took to travel from Brooklyn to Manhattan. Indeed, there was nothing stopping me from cleaning for some older people I know, one who's quite sick; both would be grateful for the help. For that matter, I could clean my mother's house next time I visited.

But would I? I looked around at the dozing Ittoenites, many clutching the small boxes of caramels that we had been given after lunch. For the first time I noticed how innocent it all seemed. A simple life, but complicated in its implications. Where would you go if you had ambition or a desire to see the world or a mind that thrived, as did Sho's, in an arena of challenging numbers?

We marched back up to the compound and were again greeted by those who had stayed behind, each standing silent, hands in prayer. Bowing. Bowing. I returned the bows.

I so much wanted to leave Ittoen, and I wanted to stay. The week's experience had set me face-to-face with my shortcomings and fears. In my cleaning world I got things —money, free time, acknowledgment. Here, cleaning was about giving everything up. The complications of my life —what to do or be, where to live—fell away against the backdrop of this selfless community. Dust to dust? Who really believes it?

My last teatime with Ayako was brief. She offered tangerines, tart and juicy.

"How can others—how can *I*—live Ittoen principles out there? In America?"

Ayako's eyes were downcast. She carefully separated the sections of her fruit and didn't say anything for what seemed a long time, though this wasn't unusual during our talks. I often felt like I asked too many questions, and the ones I asked seemed obvious when put to her.

"Live a simple life with an affluent spirit."

This was nice, though it seemed pat, like a proverb, valid but in practicality, vapid.

I sipped my tea and flipped again through my favorite photo album, the one with pictures of early Ittoen life. There were several photos of Ayako and Tenko-san cleaning together, which now, after my own cleaning experience, seemed truly beautiful. And another: Ayako with her headscarf tied behind her ears, hands laced together and barely visible over the right shoulder of an aged Tenko-san, steadying himself with a staff, the misty Ittoen hillside in the background.

"Take whatever you wish," Ayako said.

"But these are originals. You must want them?" I asked. "Others must want them?"

Silence. I touched the pictures. I really did want them.

"I'll die soon," Ayako said. "A few will be saved. The rest will burn with my body and go with the ashes of the others, with the ashes of Tenko-san."

She said this matter-of-factly, without any New Age solemnity or the pomp that might have accompanied this kind of bare-bones spiritual announcement. I peeled several photos from the book.

"Take care of everything you have," she added. "Everything given to us is in trust from the Light."

Suddenly, I thought of the place I owned in the Bay Area. Eight years ago, when I had first quit my job and set off for a writer's colony, an adventure I thought might last a year, I had sublet the house. Since then, I had lived in at least seven cities, on several continents, snagged at least a dozen sublets myself, and began my cleaning life. I knew the basement of my house was now crammed full of other people's castoffs, and the neatly tended garden was overgrown. The once bountiful fruit trees were in desperate need of husbandry and no longer producing. A tenant had recently sent me pictures of my bedroom, post-1989 earthquake; a mix of large cracks and hairline fractures criss-crossed the walls.

It was time to clean house.